John's Gospel in New Perspective

John's Gospel in New Perspective

Christology and the Realities of Roman Power

Richard J. Cassidy

ORBIS BOOKS

Maryknoll, New York 10545

Library of Congress Cataloging-in-Publication Data

Cassidy, Richard J.
    John's Gospel in new perspective : Christology and the
realities of Roman power / Richard J. Cassidy.
        p. cm.
    Includes bibliographical references.
    ISBN 0-88344-841-6 — ISBN 0-88344-818-1
    1. Bible. N.T. John — Criticism, interpretation, etc.
2. Persecution — History — Early church, ca. 30-600. I. Title.
BS2615.2.C38   1992
226.5'06 — dc20   92-2294
                                                              CIP

DEDICATION

To my parents, Vincent J. Cassidy and Bernice Larkin Cassidy, in remembrance of their fiftieth anniversary of Christian marriage, February 15, 1991.

And to Fr. Peter J. Drilling and Fr. Albert E. Kirk, friends I have valued and esteemed for over twenty-five years, friends who were graciously present for the joyous celebration of this fiftieth anniversary.

Contents

CHAPTER SIX
Jesus' Farewell Discourses

CHAPTER SEVEN
John 20-21 and Readers in Roman Surroundings

CHAPTER EIGHT
The Purposes of the Gospel of John

Preface

At the beginning of the second century, in the years around 110, the imperial emissary Pliny conducted investigations involving members of the Christian communities in Pontus, the Eastern Roman province to which he had just been appointed. At least two women ministers were tortured by Pliny in his efforts to gain information. And by his own account he actually executed a number of other Christians when they refused to renounce their allegiance to Christ.

These considerations regarding Pliny's repressive measures are particularly important to the analysis of John's Gospel that will be made in the following pages. For it is a principal thesis of the present book that John had Christians such as these in view as he worked at his Gospel. Indeed, John very much intended that his Gospel would provide encouragement and strength to those around him who were in any way threatened for their faith.

What brought me to this particular perspective regarding John's Gospel? I wish to state that I came to it as a result of a combination of graces that were afforded to me. My previous analyses of the Gospel of Luke and the Acts of the Apostles provided a platform for this interpretation of John. However, it was in reflecting upon the emperor Trajan's at once "enlightened" yet factually brutal reply to Pliny that my imagination was stirred as to the situation of John's readers.

In the later stages of writing my sensitivities regarding this aspect of John's Gospel were heightened as a consequence of having two close friends enter into circumstances in which martyrdom was a distinct possibility. I refer here to Fr. Dean Brackley, SJ, now serving in the group replacing the six Jesuits and two women of their service staff who were assassinated at the University of Central America in El Salvador in 1989. I also refer to Fr. Fred Thelen from the diocese of Lansing, Michigan, currently serving as a Maryknoll associate in the region of Peru where terrorists have actually murdered several priests and threatened the lives of other Church workers.

In addition to recognizing the witness of these friends, I wish to express gratitude to others who assisted in various ways. At several stages of my research I benefited from the service provided by Fr. Eugene Rooney, SJ, and the staff at the Woodstock Theological Library at Georgetown University in Washington, D.C. Then at various stages of the writing process I was pleased to receive warm hospitality and helpful pastoral perspective from Fr. Victor Clore, the pastor at Detroit's Christ the King parish, and from the hospitable parish staff there.

At Fordham University I benefited greatly from the cordial surroundings that were constituted on the one hand by the dedicated, congenial faculty and students of the Graduate School of Religion/RE and on the other hand by the welcoming members of the Fordham Jesuit Community and the generous staff members who serve at Loyola—Faber Hall. In particular the admirable efforts of Avery Dulles, SJ, vigorously engaged in his own book on faith at the Pistic Studies Desk, were an encouragement to me as I aspired to steady days at the Johannine Studies Desk. And by solemn agreement I am pleased to list by name the members of the Johannine Literature class for the spring semester of 1990. They are: Mathukutty Chacko (India), James R. Hoerter, You-Seon Kim (Korea), Michele M. Kroll, Karla Kivinen Layden, Marian Maskulak, CPS, James T. Roberson, and Thomas Sweeney, SDB. It is indeed a tribute both to the administration and staff of the Graduate School of Religion and to the administration of Fordham University itself that virtually every course in the GSRRE includes members from several continents and not infrequently students from *all* six of the major continents.

The nearly tripled size of the Johannine Literature course for the spring of 1991 made it possible to envision a more ambitious staging of John's Roman trial narrative. All class members served effectively in one or more capacities, but the contribution made by the person especially responsible for this endeavor should be recognized. In the framework given by her recent Christian conversion, Nina A. David initially proposed that the trial narrative of John 18-19 be treated in connection with eucharistic elements of John 21; she then subsequently directed a class performance/liturgy that strikingly and reverently integrated both dimensions. I was striving to grasp the relationship between John 21 and the Gospel proper at that time and the insights that I gained from experiencing this drama and worship service significantly enriched the presentation that is now given in chapters seven and eight below.

I wish also to acknowledge the steady encouragement given me through-out this entire research and writing process by Msgr. Bernard J. Harrington, pastor of St. Rene Goupil Parish in Sterling Heights, Michigan. For his continuing affirmation I am deeply grateful. As a priest of the Detroit Archdiocese I also wish to express my appreciation for the highly positive support that I have received for this undertaking from the two archbishops who have served the Church of Detroit during this interval—from Cardinal Edmund C. Szoka and Archbishop Adam J. Maida.

Finally, recognition is appropriately given for the work involved in turn-ing drafts into a finished manuscript and the work involved in preparing the indexes for the printed book. Regarding the latter undertaking I am appreciative of the assistance given by Leda E. Reeves, SSJ. And I espe-cially wish to recognize that she rendered this dedicated service during a period when truly remarkable courage was required of her in facing sickness within her family.

The word processing of the manuscript, at times under considerable pressure, was diligently performed by Allyson M. Larkin. As I thank her by name I am also given the opportunity to note a small aspect in connection with the dedication of this book. For in 1991 an event occurred that marked and celebrated steadiness in a kind of faith and life that is not far removed from the Gospel of John. And it is that event which still resonates in my memory.

Given the intervening years, I can only regard it as serendipitous that the woman who typed my first high school term paper also possesses the family name of Larkin. To that woman, my mother, and to my father I remain unendingly grateful. I have received at their hands, through these years, a steady stream of graces related to Christian faith.

1

Orientation to John's Gospel

In depicting Jesus' identity and mission within his Gospel, the evangelist John was concerned to present elements and themes that were especially significant for Christian readers facing Roman imperial claims and for any who faced Roman persecution. Such a statement is offered at the outset of this study as an orientation for the analysis that will be made in the chapters that follow. Even when stated in such an introductory fashion, this thesis may well prove startling for many readers and students of the Gospel of John. The reason for such surprise is simply that John's Gospel has traditionally *not* been approached with a particular sensitivity for its Roman context.[1]

John's Gospel has frequently been analyzed as a Gospel emphasizing personal belief in, and an "abiding in," Jesus. Yet may there not also be a message within the Gospel to Christians who faced significant political challenges and pressures as a result of their personal allegiance to Jesus? Within scholarly circles John's Gospel has frequently been regarded as responding to Hellenistic culture, to Gnosticism, and to the rupture between Judaism and Christianity.[2] But, apart from these considerations, may it not be the case that the Gospel consciously responds to significant developments within the Roman world? To express these questions in such a manner serves to advance the view that John was influenced by multiple cares and concerns when he published his Gospel. Simultaneously, such questions also emphasize the new insight that Roman actions and policies were significant influences upon John at the time when he published his account.

In effect, then, what is signalled by these questions is the intention of achieving a modification in the conceptual scaffolding traditionally used to investigate the various dimensions of John's Gospel. While the presently existing scaffolding is extremely useful, it is far from comprehensive. In particular, the present scaffolding needs to be expanded with new materials and perspectives derived from considering features of the Gospel that relate extraordinarily well to significant elements in Roman rule at the end of the first Christian century and the beginning of the second century.

1. THE AUTHORSHIP OF JOHN'S GOSPEL

Within contemporary New Testament studies there are scarcely more disputed topics than those pertaining to the composition and authorship of John's Gospel. The traditional view is that the present twenty-one chapters of the Gospel were written by a single person, a member of Jesus' group of apostles. However, many recent interpretations have disputed this view and have, in the main, posited a much more complex process of composition, one involving a redactor (editor) in addition to the initial writer and quite probably the contributions of others as well.

Readers of the present study who wish to investigate the question of authorship at greater depth should give their attention to the discussions of the subject that can be found in virtually all of the leading commentaries on John's Gospel.[3] The same recommendation is also made in regard to the much discussed subject of the sources that may have been utilized in the composition of the Gospel.[4] However, at this juncture, the point to be grasped in relation to the present study is that its principal thesis is fundamentally compatible with either the traditional or the more recent views regarding the authorship of the Gospel.

The rationale for such an assertion has essentially to do with the fact that, whatever the exact process of composition, John's Gospel eventually reached a final form and began to be circulated within the early Christian community. Conceivably, a single author may have written the Gospel out of personal energy and inspiration. Conceivably, one writer may have written a draft of the present Gospel with the prologue (1:1-18), other passages, and an appendix (21:1-25) supplied by a later editor-publisher. Conceivably, other members of a "Johannine school" may also have been substantially involved in the process. Nevertheless, at some stage, the Gospel achieved its final form and began to be read as a finished account.

The image of a scroll or codex containing the Gospel being formally prepared for circulation is perhaps a useful image to adduce here.[5] At some point in time someone with ultimate responsibility for the text made the decision that the Gospel was now finished and took steps to circulate it within the surrounding Christian community. Within the present study, the person who took these steps will henceforward be referred to as "John" or as "the evangelist." Once again, this person (or persons) may have become involved in the authorship of the Gospel after another (others) had already written the major portions of what is now the finished Gospel. However, on the other hand it must not be precluded that the person who finalized the Gospel was indeed the very person who composed it from the beginning. In any event, humanly speaking, *John* is now named as the person who ultimately determined what perspectives regarding Jesus' identity and mission would reach the first readers of the Fourth Gospel.

2. THE DATE OF JOHN'S GOSPEL

At what date did John finalize his Gospel and commend it to his readers? On this question contemporary scholarly opinion is widely diversified with a few scholars on one end of the spectrum favoring a date as early as 65 C.E. and a few on the other end arguing for dates as far into the second century as 130. Perhaps it is safe to say that the preponderance of scholarly opinion favors a date somewhere within the last decade of the first century, i.e., a date between 90 and 100 C.E. Yet even scholars who advance plausible reasons for regarding this decade as the most probable time of composition are careful to leave open the possibility that John may have completed his work on either side of that decade.

Significantly, just as the central thesis of the present study is congruent with a single or multiple-author theory of composition, so is it also generally compatible with virtually all of the views traditionally expressed regarding the Gospel's date of publication. For, as will be indicated in chapters two and three, the Roman policies and procedures that this study asserts as influences upon John were substantially in place from the decade of the 70s onwards.[6]

Nevertheless, these considerations relative to general compatibility should not be taken to mean that there are not intervals within the spectrum of dates that are more congenial to the thesis of this study. As will be seen below, developments highly relevant to John's final account occurred during the reigns of the Roman emperors Domitian (81-96) and Trajan (98-117). And thus, if it can be established on other grounds that John published his account sometime after the early 80s, additional grounding will be available for the principal argument being advanced here. Still, it must be noted that definite evidence concerning Trajan's decision that Christians be executed "for the name" does not preclude the possibility that the execution of Christians on comparable grounds had already taken place many years earlier.

3. THE LOCATION OF JOHN AND HIS READERS

If it can be said that there is a certain clustering of scholarly opinion around the decade of the 90s as the likely date of John's work, it can also be said that there is a certain convergence of scholarly opinion in favor of Ephesus as the most likely location for the Gospel. On what grounds is Ephesus so favored? Usually a judgment about the Gospel's place is influenced by elements within the text that presumably congrue well with the known features of a particular location. In addition the testimony supplied from external sources, e.g., Irenaeus and other early Christian writers, may well be utilized.[7]

In addition to Ephesus other locations that have been advanced include Antioch in Syria, Alexandria in Egypt, and a location within Palestine. Each of these other locations does have adherents and, given the paucity of incontrovertible evidence, it hardly seems possible to move beyond relative grades of plausibility in seeking to identify John's exact location.[8]

Within the framework of the present study, though, it is not John's exact location, but rather his *general* location that is of inestimable importance! For, as can easily be determined from a brief glance at the map on page 92, Ephesus itself as well as Antioch, Alexandria, and the Palestinian territories are *all* located within the confines of the Roman empire. Stating this point virtually borders upon stating a truism. Yet this fundamental insight is critical for the interpretation of the Gospel that will be advanced in the succeeding chapters.

Where was John located? It is unassailable that John was not located in Parthia or Dacia or anywhere else outside of the boundaries of the Roman empire. In contrast, what can immediately be said of the territories of Asia, Syria, Judea, and Egypt is that, at the time of John's work, they all were located within the territories ruled by Rome. And thus, wherever John's location when he published his Gospel, he published it within the geographical and political context of Roman rule.

What is more, as incontrovertibly as John himself is to be located within the context of Roman rule, so too are his intended readers. Did John envision his Gospel as a resource for the Christians and potential Christians of one locality only? Or rather, did he envision it as a document that would serve Christians and those proximate to Christianity wherever they were located? Did John supervise the production of copies of the Gospel for use outside of the locality in which he himself resided? Posing such questions as these serves to emphasize again that the Roman empire is both the venue for the Gospel and the venue for its readers.

At this point it is also important to reflect again upon the reality of John's Gospel as a document that *circulated*.[9] John, located somewhere within the empire, circulated the Gospel as an authoritative document to readers who were located with him in one province of the empire, but also to readers located in the adjacent provinces.

What this means, obviously, is that John and his readers both possessed a common frame of reference as to the various facets and the basic patterns of Roman rule. For both John and his readers, Roman provincial rule was a common experience. For both John and his readers, Roman political and military procedures were understood realities. And for both John and his readers, the initiatives of a new emperor, or even those of a new governor, were very definitely phenomena to be reckoned with.

4. THE STRUCTURE OF THE PRESENT STUDY

From the foregoing considerations the basic rationale for the present study should now be evident and it remains to indicate the principal structural lines of the chapters that follow. Initially there will be two chapters delineating important imperial practices in the approximate time frame of John's Gospel. These brief chapters will then be followed by four chapters in which passages in John's account that seem to respond to these Roman realities will be analyzed. The final chapter of the book will then summarize the intervening analysis and state, in developed form, the thesis of this study.

Readers should be cautioned at this juncture, a caution that will be explained more fully at the outset of chapter four, not to expect that definitive empirical proof will be given to establish that John consciously responded to the realities of Roman rule in setting forth his Gospel. Rather, what will be illuminated is (a) that John's Gospel generally responds to the phenomena of Roman claims and Roman persecution with extraordinary effectiveness and (b) that particular features and elements of the Gospel have a truly amazing congruence with key terms and key practices that the Roman authorities utilized in their governance and in their dealings with Christians.

2

The Jewish Tax and the Cult of Rome's Emperors

This chapter will treat two phenomena that are significant for the subject of Christian existence under Roman rule. With respect to John's Gospel, the phenomenon of the *imperial cult* is certainly of far greater consequence. However, in an effort to convey an enhanced appreciation for the character of first-century relations among Romans, Jews, and Christians, an analysis of the so named *Jewish Tax* will also be made.

Before embarking upon this analysis it is important to indicate the time intervals that are involved. With respect to the inception of the Jewish Tax and its first implementation, the era of the Flavian emperors (69-96 C.E.) is clearly of central importance, particularly the reign of Domitian (81-96). Then, recognizing the significant reform in the administration of this tax under Nerva, the interval for consideration is appropriately expanded to include the two years of Nerva's reign (96-98) and the ensuing years of his successor Trajan (98-117).

With respect to the phenomenon of the imperial cult the appropriate time span is evidently broader and in a fully comprehensive analysis would begin systematically in 31 B.C.E. with the reign of Augustus. Yet such an extended span of time is beyond the limits of the present study and, accordingly, more concentrated attention will be given to the emperors whose reigns are closest to the presumed time of John's Gospel. In effect, this means that Domitian and Trajan will receive comparatively extended treatment although mention will be made of the use of such titles as "lord" and "savior of the world" by Nero and those preceding him.

1. ASPECTS OF THE JEWISH TAX

Inasmuch as he was the one who initiated it, it is appropriate to begin consideration of the Jewish Tax with Vespasian.[1] From the standpoint of Roman-Jewish-Christian relations, it is of considerable significance that

Vespasian was the general commanding the Roman forces charged with crushing the Jewish revolt of 66 C.E. When events within the empire resulted in his being acclaimed as emperor in 69, he entrusted the final stages of the Judean campaign to his son Titus and returned to Rome in triumph. Titus, for his part, achieved a particularly savage destruction of Jerusalem, including the Jerusalem temple. He then also returned to Rome, there to have standing along with his ambitious younger brother, Domitian, as presumed heir to his father's throne.

This skeletal description of the events by which the rule of the Roman empire devolved to Vespasian and his two sons nevertheless makes it possible to appreciate that Vespasian and Titus would be interested in highlighting their military successes in order to enhance their credentials for holding the emperorship. And in point of fact, the Flavians and their supporters did engage in a variety of undertakings designed to ensure that their accomplishments in crushing the Jewish revolt would be widely and enduringly recognized. To this end architectural commemorations such as the Arch of Titus were commissioned and, to this end, coins depicting a rebellious Judea prostrate before Rome were minted and widely circulated.[2] In the same vein, the captured Jewish historian Josephus was given latitude to compose a history of the entire Jewish war, a history stressing the foolhardiness of opposition to Roman dominion and the accomplishments of the Roman generals, Vespasian and Titus.

By reason of his direct involvement in crushing the Jewish uprising, Vespasian was personally familiar with the various aspects of the situation in Judea and (in reference to the present topic) knowledgeable regarding the dedication with which Jews in Judea and elsewhere contributed annually to the support of the Jerusalem temple. This practice was a remarkable one. The amount of the annual contribution was fixed at a didrachma and it was contributed by all male Jews of twenty-one years and older.[3] So well established had this practice become that previous emperors had directed governors of the various provinces not to impede the collection and transportation of these monies from their respective provinces to Jerusalem.[4]

And now the Jerusalem temple laid in ruins, plundered and leveled by Titus in the final days once the Jerusalem city walls had been successfully breached. For Jews throughout the empire as well as for those in Jerusalem and its environs, what an unspeakable tragedy! For the conquering Romans and certainly for Vespasian, however, was this not an event to be exploited still more fully? Why should the rebellious Jews of Syria-Judea and those throughout the empire who had sympathized with them not be taught an additional lesson as to the full costs of rising against Roman sovereignty? Why should the Romans themselves, having already plundered the treasury and the artifacts of the temple, not avail themselves of an opportunity for realizing a continuing stream of plunder as the fruit of a campaign that had proven so costly?

Presumably taking account of these and related considerations, Vespasian acted shortly after Titus had crushed the remaining Jewish resistance and promulgated a new imperial edict stipulating that a tax was to be levied upon all Jews for the support of the temple of Jupiter on the Capitoline Hill in Rome![5]

From the point of view of the Roman conquerors and the new emperor Vespasian, such a step could be regarded as a near stroke of genius. Jews throughout the empire already had the custom of contributing two drachmas to the Jerusalem temple. Now, to teach them enduringly as to the futility of challenges against Roman rule, they would have to send the same amount annually to Rome. Since Jews were already accustomed to budget two drachmas for this extra-domestic purpose, it could not be argued that it was impossible for them to pay the new tax. And what a significant financial boon both to the finances and the stature of the new emperor. Indeed, so significant was this new tax expected to be that there was need to establish a separate treasury in Rome in order to oversee its administration. And so, the Fiscus Judaicus was established by imperial decree as the administrative center for this new tax upon the empire's Jews.

Yet who were encompassed within the designation of *all* Jews? It is at this point that the interest of the present study to conjecture regarding the impact that the Jewish tax had upon the new Christian movement comes to the fore. It is also at this point that initiatives undertaken by Domitian in the matter of this tax emerge for consideration.

In assessing the comprehensiveness of Vespasian's tax, it must be asked whether it extended to those who had not been born Jews but later became converts to Judaism. Second, it must be asked whether it applied to those who had been born Jews but later rejected the Jewish religion and Jewish religious practices. Third, it must also be asked whether it applied to born Jews who now considered themselves members of the new Christian movement, a movement sometimes regarded as a "sect" within Judaism, albeit one with numerous Gentile members. Presumably Vespasian at the very least intended the tax for those who had previously paid two drachmas annually to the Jerusalem temple. However, given the socio-religious circumstances in which this tax was imposed, it must have been bitterly resented. As a consequence, virtually every form of justification for non-payment would be advanced.

For the reigns of Vespasian (69-79) and Titus (79-81) sufficient data is not present to justify even so much as a tentative answer to any of the questions posed above. With respect to the reign of Domitian, the data is scarcely more plentiful. However, when one relatively extended report by the contemporary writer Suetonius is read in conjunction with the evidence afforded by the inscriptions on coins minted by the next emperor, Nerva, it is possible to conclude that Domitian enforced this tax much more rigorously than his father or brother did. It is also possible to conclude on the basis of this evidence that, as a consequence of Domitian's vigorous enforcement, public interrogations of Jews and those suspected of being Jews occurred on a wide scale.

Several aspects of the statement that Suetonius includes in his essay on Domitian should be noted at the outset. (See below for the text of this passage.) The first aspect is that, because of his desperation over the depleted imperial treasuries, Domitian was "very vigorously" (*acerbissime*) enforcing the payment of this tax. The second and third aspects regard the two groups that now came under increased scrutiny for payment of the tax. One group consisted of those who lived as Jews without publicly acknowledging that they were Jews. The other group consisted of born Jews who claimed not to be Jewish.

Although it is impossible to have certainty regarding the identity of those who constituted either of these groups, the distinct possibility that Christians may have been included in the first group designated by Suetonius should not be overlooked. On this reading Gentiles who became Christians began in a way to "live as Jews." While the process by which male Gentiles converted to Christianity did not require their circumcision, they were nevertheless embracing a way of life that closely resembled Judaism in its other aspects. This being the case, it can be surmised that outsiders would have had a considerable amount of difficulty in distinguishing them from practicing Jews.

It is significant (and a further indication of how difficult it is to reconstruct the actual situation) that some commentators have also located Christians within the *second* group that Suetonius designates, those who were born Jews yet "concealed their origin" for purposes of avoiding payment of the tax.[6] Surely it is conceivable that born Jews who converted to Christianity may have adopted the view that their new Christian identity exempted them from the payment of this tax. And thus, for example, even if a man had been circumcised in accordance with Jewish law, had practiced as a Jew throughout most of his life, and had annually made the contribution to the Jerusalem temple, still, having recently become a Christian, he might now conceivably resist any payment of the officially designated *Jewish* Tax to Jupiter's temple.

At this juncture it can easily be envisioned just how vulnerable to abuse Domitian's program for a more rigorous collection of the Jewish Tax actually was. Imagine the situation of Roman officials faced with having to decide whether certain individuals were actually "Jewish enough" to have a responsibility for paying the tax. Concomitantly, was it not by means of informers and as a result of public denunciations that instances of alleged tax evasion would frequently come to the attention of these officials?

It is now appropriate to consider the full report given by Suetonius regarding this situation. Note that in addition to delineating the two categories of people now prosecuted, Suetonius indicates the incredible extremes to which the concern to establish Jewish identity could be taken:

Besides other taxes, that on the Jews were levied with the utmost rigor and those were prosecuted who without publicly acknowledging that faith yet lived as Jews as well as those who concealed their origin and did not pay the tribute levied upon their people. I recall being present in my youth when the person of a man ninety years old was examined before the procurator and in a very crowded court, to see if he was circumcised (*Domitian* 12.2).

In the section of this chapter concerning the imperial ruler cult, it will be seen that Domitian was guilty of arrogance and excesses that are astounding even when viewed against the backdrop of the incredibly exorbitant practices of some of the emperors who preceded him, e.g., Gaius and Nero. However, judging from the public repudiation of Domitian's practices regarding the Jewish Tax that Nerva made, there is a sound basis for surmising that extraordinary abuses must have occurred.

For how else to interpret the fact the Nerva, shortly after coming to power, had a new set of brass coins minted, coins bearing the Latin inscription *FISCI IUDAICI CALUMNIA SUBLATA*. The conciseness of this inscription is difficult to capture in English translation. Nevertheless, a near approximation of what it announced would be: "The Abolition of the Vexatious Exaction of the Tax on the Jews."[7]

Since the letters *S. C.* (standing for *Senatus Consultum* and indicating a resolution of the Roman Senate) also appear on the surface of the coin, it is clear that there was a broad-based conviction that the abuses that had existed under Domitian had to be ended. Again, it must be emphasized that these abuses must have been occurring extensively throughout the empire. Why else go through the trouble of such an auspicious means of communication as imperial coinage? Inasmuch as practicing Jews were widely dispersed throughout the territories of the empire (at this time, presumably to a lesser degree, so were practicing Christians), there was in fact a rationale for such a universal measure.

With respect to the time interval that is of concern within the present study, it is significant to note that the decision taken by Nerva in this matter did not end the collection of the Jewish Tax. For what Nerva and the Roman Senate were addressing was not the tax itself but the abusive collection practices that the tax occasioned. What Nerva thus effected was a reform in the practices surrounding the tax and not the end of the tax itself.[8] Indeed, surviving tax records establish that the Jewish Tax continued to be collected during Nerva's reign and well beyond it.[9]

2. THE CULT OF ROME'S EMPERORS

As an initial orientation to the analysis of this section, it is useful to note that within the Gospel of John Jesus is addressed/acclaimed by three titles that were appropriated by one or more of the Roman emperors who reigned in the middle and ending decades of the first century. What was the context in which these titles were appropriated by such figures as Nero, Vespasian, Titus, and especially by Domitian? The paragraphs that immediately follow will consider the general setting in which these titles were utilized. This brief overview will then be followed by a more focused analysis of the three titles in question.

A. Practices Associated with the Imperial Cult

Any attempt to describe something as complex as the practices and claims associated with the cult of the Roman emperors within the confines of a few paragraphs will always be a somewhat perilous undertaking. Thus readers should recognize that only a highly generalized analysis can be given within the space available.[10] This analysis is thus more designed to alert readers to significant aspects of the situation than it is to set forth a comprehensive explanation treating every feature of this complex phenomenon.

One way of interpreting the first-century materials pertaining to the conduct of various emperors is to view the situation in terms of political survival. Here it should be recalled that the office of emperor had only come into existence after Augustus had defeated his various rivals through civil war and had skillfully achieved a working relationship with the Roman Senate and the people of Rome. By reason of Augustus' various achievements the role of his successors was strengthened, yet they too faced recurring challenges and looked for ways of consolidating their positions and their influence.

At this juncture attention is appropriately directed to the amorphous, complex Greco-Roman system of the gods. This system, in existence long before the time of Augustus and his successors, was nevertheless susceptible to manipulation and modification by the emperors themselves as well as by other persons of influence from the provinces and in Rome. Indeed, so many political factors were intertwined with so many religious factors that it is extremely difficult to delineate the boundary between these two dimensions.

Two examples of modifications in this system are appropriately mentioned here as developments that tended to strengthen the position of the emperor. The first innovation to be noted is that by which Augustus and his more illustrious successors and came to be venerated as supra-human. The term *divus* was the term used of these emperors. Literally its meaning is "divine." There is, however, a significant distinction between this term and *deus*, "a god."

While standing as *divus* was something only conferred upon an emperor after his death and, while it was not a recognition bestowed upon every emperor, the significance of this step for those who were later in the succession must not be overlooked. For if one or more of one's predecessors was "divine," was not something of that aura thereby conferred upon the present occupant of the imperial throne?

The second innovation that served to advance the sovereign position of the ruling emperor was the fact that, particularly in the eastern provinces, the custom was fostered of blending a certain kind of worship of the *living* emperor with the more established forms of worship of the city of Rome and its majesty. Thus various temples and shrines honoring the reigning emperor came to be built and sacrifices seem to have been offered *for* Rome and *for* the living emperor; however, at least in some instances, the sacrifices were actually *to* a particular emperor.

Clearly external conditions within Rome and her provinces always exercised an influence upon the way in which an emperor inclined to claim supra-human standing and sovereignty might proceed to advance his claims. Nevertheless, given the system that was in effect, it is not difficult to imagine an emperor with the mentality and personality of a Gaius, a Nero, or a Domitian pressing such claims to the limit. Indeed, their untempered claims were sometimes such that many who viewed the Roman imperial system itself with favor could only disdain these excesses.

Before closing this stage of the study and moving to an analysis of the three imperial titles, one more element pertaining to the imperial cult should be considered. This particular practice is documented for the reign of Trajan, but it can be plausibly suggested that it originally developed under Domitian or was at least inspired by some of Domitian's comparable practices.[11] The practice in question is the procedure by which those accused of disloyalty to the emperor or of neglecting the Roman religion could exculpate themselves from such charges.

The correspondence between Trajan and Pliny, his special legate for the province of Bithynia-Pontus, will be considered at length in the following chapter. However, it is effective in this context to cite Pliny's description of one of the tests that he employed for confirming that some of those denounced to him were *not* Christians. One part of Pliny's procedure was to have such persons offer incense and wine before the Roman gods and then before the image of Trajan himself. Pliny does not indicate the origins of this test; it cannot be ruled out that he himself originated it. However, as suggested above, such a procedure does have "the aura of Domitian" about it, and it is plausible to conjecture that, directly or indirectly, Domitian was the source of it.

Significantly, Trajan does not specifically address this aspect in his relatively brief reply. Nevertheless, his letter is phrased in such a way as to indicate that he accepted the validity of the procedure for testing that Pliny had utilized. Such acceptance indicates that even an emperor often regarded as "moderate" gave tacit endorsement to a practice that tended to bestow supra-human status upon him. And thus, even if Domitian was the originator of this particular loyalty test, it is significant that figures of the stature of Trajan and Pliny displayed their willingness to proceed in terms of it.

B. Three Significant Imperial Titles

As indicated in the paragraphs opening this section, three titles associated with the imperial cult also appear within the final text of John's Gospel and thereby assume major significance in terms of the present study. These titles are "Savior of the world," "Lord," and "Lord and God." It will be the task of the paragraphs that follow to provide a basic perspective on each of them with particular attention devoted to "Lord and God" owing to the prominent position this title occupies in the concluding verses of John 20.

As was indicated for the previously considered elements pertaining to the imperial cult, comprehensive data are not presently available for establishing the precise use of the given titles by the emperors of this period. Inscriptions of various kinds and various forms of literary evidence are the two principal extant sources of information about such usage. However, given the extended interval under consideration and the extensive territories encompassed within the empire, it is perhaps not surprising that, in several cases, little more than the fact of usage can be established. Nevertheless, even this skeletal information can be extremely useful in terms of the present analysis.

Such considerations have particular relevance in reference to the various ways in which the Roman emperors were heralded as saviors. The first Roman leader to be acclaimed simply as "savior" was Julius Caesar. Subsequently, however, this title was used unadorned or else in combination with adulatory modifiers for the following emperors: Augustus, Tiberius, Claudius, Nero, Vespasian, Titus, Trajan, and Hadrian.[12]

What can be said precisely concerning the title "savior of the world"? It is noteworthy that on the inscriptions that have survived, the use of this exact title is attested for only two emperors. (Again, this does not preclude new discoveries establishing that the title was bestowed on and prized by others as well.) Hadrian, who was also referred to more simply as "savior," is one of the two. Strictly speaking, though, his reign (117-138) lies outside the time interval presently under consideration.

What other emperor is so designated? It is of more that casual significance that the other emperor acclaimed by this title is none other than Nero (54-68). In Nero's case the extant inscriptions amply document that, upon his accession to the imperial throne, the dramatic title used to herald him in the Eastern regions of the empire was "savior of the world."[13]

The *extensive* use of the term "lord" as a title conferring supra-human status upon an emperor also seems to date from Nero's reign. For Egypt perhaps fifty years earlier there are papyrus temple accounts that mention sacrifices for "the god and lord emperor," a reference to Augustus.[14] And records of various kinds also indicate the use of "lord" for Tiberius, Gaius, and Claudius.[15] Nevertheless, the existing evidence suggests that there was a remarkable upsurge in the use of this term during Nero's reign, primarily but not exclusively in the Eastern provinces.[16]

Moving from the time of Nero to the era of Hadrian, the extant data reveal a continuing use of "lord" as a means of indicating the exalted standing and identity of the ruling emperor. Pottery fragments testify to the use of this title for Vespasian and Domitian[17] and continued use of "lord" can also be established for the regimes of Trajan and Hadrian.[18] In several respects Trajan seems to have been concerned to retreat from the excesses of Domitian. Nevertheless, he clearly remained favorable to being addressed as "lord" and also acquiesced in other comparable titles. Indeed it will be seen below that Pliny, in keeping with his generally obsequious patterns, addressed Trajan as "lord."

Remarkably, when attention is finally directed to the Roman emperors' use of "lord and god," the third title that is present within the Gospel of John, the focus narrows to the rule of just one emperor, Domitian. Seemingly Domitian stood alone among those who came before and after him in sanctioning, and even in demanding, this particular term of supra-human claim.[19]

Given the importance of this title within John's Gospel it is worth delving in some detail into Domitian's attempted self exaltation by means of it. Here the sources for attestation are primarily literary. Alongside two inscriptions that have survived, there are three contemporary authors (Suetonius, Martial, and Dio Chrysostom) and one third-century historian (Dio Cassius) whose works document Domitian's self-aggrandizing use of this title.

In assessing the personality and reign of the early emperors in his work, *Lives of the Caesars*, Suetonius obviously has a disdain for Domitian, and that fact should be considered in considering his various reports regarding Domitian's career. Still, unless what Suetonius has written is to be regarded as a total fabrication, his statement that Domitian referred to himself in a formal decree as "our lord and our god" (*Dominus et Deus Noster*) constitutes an important datum. Earlier in his account Suetonius had reported that Domitian delighted to hear the people in the amphitheater acclaim both him and his wife as "lords" (*Dominus et Domina*). Suetonius then supplies this account regarding the decree Domitian published arrogating "lord and god" to his own person:

> With not less arrogance he began as follows in issuing a circular letter in the name of his procurators, "Our Lord and our God bids that this be done." And so the custom arose of henceforth addressing him in no other way even in writing or in conversation (*Domitian* 13.2).

Suetonius, Dio Chrysostom, and Dio Cassius all wrote as historians, but testimony about Domitian's practices is also given epigrammatically by Martial, a satirist from the province of Spain writing in Rome during the last decades of the first century. In the epigrams that Martial published while Domitian reigned, there is one especially significant reference to an edict "of our lord and god" and there are also two other cases in which this title appears in his writings. However, it is after Domitian's murder that Martial's most telling reference appears.

Apparently, once Domitian's reign was over and more "moderate" emperors replaced him, Martial began to have second thoughts about his own excesses as a sychophant. And thus, perhaps to express his misgivings but perhaps also to ingratiate himself with those who now ruled, Martial published the following repudiation of his former practice of addressing Domitian as "lord and god." Note that Martial now affirms that there is no one who should be addressed in such a way. And note also that he ingratiatingly attempts to excuse his past lapses as having been due to the influence of "the Flatteries," stating that since then he has not been swayed by them:

In vain, O ye Flatteries, ye come to me, wretched creatures with your shameless lips; I think not to address any man as Lord and God (*Epigrams* 10.72.1-3).

The third ancient writer whose testimony against Domitian's "lord and god" excesses has been preserved is Dio Chrysostom. In the passage now to be cited Dio writes in Greek and thus *despotēn kai theon* is the title that he decries. Significantly, he states that this was the title that "all Greeks and barbarians" proffered to this man.

And who is the ruler in question? Clearly it is Domitian. For this passage (*Discourses* 45,1) is excerpted from a speech that Dio gave in his native province of Bithynia probably in the year 102. Domitian was now dead, and Dio is emphasizing that the hardships he himself recently suffered were due to "the most powerful, most stern man" who was truly "an evil demon" despite the fact that he was popularly acclaimed as being a lord and god:

And besides all this, bearing up under the hatred, not of this or that one among my equals . . . but rather of the most powerful, most stern man, who was called by all Greeks and barbarians both lord and god but who was in reality an evil demon.

As mentioned Dio Cassius, the fourth ancient writer who testifies on this subject, was not a contemporary of Domitian but rather wrote well over one hundred years later. For that reason the first of his two reports may be based on one or more of the reports supplied by the earlier writers:

For he [Domitian] even insisted upon being regarded as a god and took vast pride in being called "lord" and "god." These titles were used not merely in speech but also in written documents (*Roman History, Epitome of Book* 67:67.4.75).

Regardless of how this first passage is to be valued, Dio's second report on this topic is certainly of far greater consequence. What follows is Dio's description of how one Juventius Celsus succeeded in gaining clemency from Domitian by repeatedly calling upon him as "lord and god." Dio presumably understands the episode in question to have occurred about the year 91:

> When he was on the point of being condemned, he begged that he might speak to the emperor in private, and thereupon did obeisance before him and after repeatedly calling him "lord" and "god" (terms that were already being applied to him by others), he said: "I have done nothing of this sort, but if I obtain a respite, I will pry into everything and will not only bring information against many persons for you but also secure their conviction." He was released on this condition, but he did not report anyone; instead, by advancing different excuses at different times, he lived until the death of Domitian (*Roman History, Epitome of Book* 67:67.13.4).

3

Pliny, Trajan, and the Christians of Pontus

Within the framework of the Roman provincial system the northern lands of Asia Minor adjacent to the Black Sea, territories within the boundaries of modern-day Turkey, constituted the province of Bithynia-Pontus. It was to this area that, in about 110 C.E., the emperor Trajan sent his experienced and trusted emissary, Gaius Plinius Caecilius Secundus, commonly known as Pliny the younger.

It was for the purpose of restoring financial and administrative order which had deteriorated within the province that Trajan sent Pliny and he entrusted him with the full range of powers that proconsuls normally possessed.[1] With reference to the subject matter of the last chapter it should also be observed that Trajan's selection of Pliny gave him not only a highly competent administrator but also someone whose loyalty at times bordered on adulation. As previously indicated, although Pliny decried Domitian's excesses, he still consistently addressed Trajan as "lord." What is more, he stated that Trajan should be deified [2] upon his death and implied that the living Trajan was already to be numbered among the gods.[3]

There were various issues to be addressed in Bithynia-Pontus during the year and a half that Pliny served there; and, as his numerous letters to Trajan and Trajan's replies (rescripts) indicate, Pliny conscientiously sought to administer in accordance with the emperor's policies and wishes. Thus, for example, Pliny writes to secure Trajan's decision on such matters as municipal expenditures, regional building projects, and the assignment of Roman troops.[4] And so also does he write to seek Trajan's approval for the approach that he has followed in dealing with cases involving the denunciation of Christians in Pontus.

To be precise, Pliny sought Trajan's decision in the matter of the Pontus Christians in the letter now designated X.96 in the collection of his correspondence, *Letters* (*Epistulae*), and he received it in the rescript now designated X.97. These two documents, both probably written around 110,[5] constitute the earliest *pagan* communication regarding the new Christian movement and thus have great significance. Indeed, from a close scrutiny

17

of the two letters, it is possible to derive important information about Christian life and Christian loyalty, about the challenges that Christians faced because of this loyalty, and also regarding the attitudes and procedures of the highest Roman officials in dealing with Christians.

It should be noted that the analysis now to be made does not intend to treat Pliny's letter (or Trajan's) in a paragraph by paragraph fashion. Instead, in an effort to highlight what the letter reveals about the situation of the Christians of Bithynia-Pontus, that aspect is treated systematically at the beginning drawing upon comments that Pliny makes at various places in his letter. Also, although the topic of the Christians' liturgical practices is of interest and Pliny's reports about them intriguing, that topic, save for one specific report, cannot be treated in the present context.

This specific report regarding the Christian liturgical gatherings is, however, appropriately considered at the outset. For what Pliny learns from questioning apostates and apparently confirms from the torture of two deaconesses is that the Christians gathered regularly on a fixed day of the week and "chanted verses . . . in honor of Christ *as if to a god*."[6] This is Pliny's language, of course, and represents a description of Christian practice from outside of the community of faith, indeed from the perspective of an official who has had these same Christians denounced to him for punishment.

1. THE OFFENSES OF CHRISTIANS

Why were Christians in Pontus being denounced to Pliny? This question is clearly significant. In a stanza at the end of his letter Pliny mentions that, as a result of his intervention against the Christians, the pagan temples are being reinvigorated and an upsurge in the sales of the flesh of sacrificial animals has occurred.[7] It is thus conceivable that those responsible for, and benefiting from, the practices attendant to the pagan temples had taken the lead in the denunciations. Secondly, inasmuch as an anonymous pamphlet had been circulated, there may also have been allegations that the Christians were engaged in *criminal* activities. However, after his investigation and interrogations, Pliny himself seems to have concluded that the denounced Christians were not guilty of crimes in the usual sense of that term.

In fact, the principal charge that seems ultimately to have been leveled against the Christians was simply that they were . . . Christians! To put this matter from the standpoint of the Christians, an *accusatio nominis*, an "accusation of the name," was being made against them. They were being denounced essentially because they were Christians and professed an allegiance to the person and the name of Jesus. After his investigation Pliny came to appreciate that this was the central issue and he specifically asked Trajan to clarify whether Christians must be punished *for being Christian* even if they were not engaging in other forms of unacceptable behavior.[8]

At this juncture the question that immediately suggests itself is: At what point in time did it become a punishable offense for someone to profess Christian allegiance? And once this question is raised, the entire subject of persecutions against Christians in the Roman empire is also raised—a subject regarding which presently unresolvable differences exist.[9] There is some basis for positing a persecution of Christians by Nero in Rome around 65 C.E. And there is also some basis for attributing a significant persecution against Christians to Domitian. At least Christian writings from a later time carry such reports, and Tacitus, the second-century Roman historian, writes that Nero launched a persecution against the Christians of Rome in the aftermath of the great fire in 65 C.E. Yet on the other hand, scholars are not lacking to question the sources and hence the reliability of these historians and to argue that prior to the third century no widespread persecution of the Christians can be established securely.

Within Pliny's letter there is another reference which sheds light on this matter, however. It is Pliny's opening explanation to Trajan that because he, Pliny, has never been present at the trials (*cognitionibus*) of Christians, he is somewhat uncertain about the appropriate procedures and the punishments to be given. In the first place, such a statement points to the fact that *formal trials* have been held previously.[10] Moreover, in making it, Pliny assumes that Trajan (a) knows about these trials and (b) has some knowledge of the procedures followed and the punishments meted out in connection with them.

Under whose reigns did the trials to which Pliny refers take place? Presumably these trials must have occurred during Domitian's reign or at the beginning of Trajan's. Pliny's phrasing implies that they occurred sometime during the period of his own public career.[11] A second legitimate inference may well be that these trials were held in Rome. As mentioned, they might have been held in the earlier years of Trajan's own reign, but arguing against this interpretation is the consideration that Pliny is essentially setting the matter before Trajan as if it were not a subject on which Trajan had previously formed his own opinion.

Pliny is confident that Trajan has a perspective on this matter. Yet he does not refer to any previous enactment or edict by Trajan when he asks the emperor to review the steps that he, Pliny, has taken. Supposing that Nerva's brief and mild rule makes such events less likely for 96-97, what then emerges as most probable is that these trials were held during the era of Domitian. Again, Pliny's phrasing indicates that Trajan knew that these trials were occurring. And, he seems to imply that Trajan possesses a better knowledge than Pliny as to the issues that were involved in these trials.

2. PLINY'S INITIAL MEASURES AGAINST CHRISTIANS

Pliny had not, however, refrained from acting in the matter of the denounced Christians until he had been in communication with Trajan on the subject. Indeed, it can be said that he was fairly deeply engaged with the situation before he sought Trajan's direction and counsel. First, as has already been indicated above, Pliny had tortured two Christian women trying to extract information from them. Second, Pliny had gone even farther and had executed a number of Christians after they persisted in maintaining their Christian witness. And third, Pliny had also implemented a set of procedures for dealing with those who, under his examination, claimed to have left Christianity earlier, i.e. apostate Christians.

That Pliny proceeded with such severity as to order the execution of those who persevered in their Christian faith can initially jolt readers who are proceeding along in Pliny's *Letters* admiring the sensibilities and the sense of responsibility that, in other matters, the new emissary exhibits.[12] Yet that, startlingly, is what Pliny himself indicates in the following passage:

> For the moment this is the line I have taken with all persons brought before me on the charge of being Christians. I have asked them in person if they are Christians; and if they admit it, I repeat the question a second and a third time, with a warning of the punishment awaiting them. *If they persist, I order them to be led away for execution* (*Letters* X.96,3; italics added).

Note that in this passage the fundamental issue is simply whether or not the denounced Christians persevere in affirming their faith commitment. Those denounced to him for trial are given three opportunities for changing their mind. If they persist, execution by the sword is then the outcome.[13]

From Pliny's brief comments it is hardly possible to estimate the numbers of Christians who suffered martyrdom under him. From his viewpoint, it was an important consideration that, in addition to ordinary provincials, there were also numbers of Roman citizens who stood firm as Christians. Since capital charges against citizens were normally to be adjudicated before the imperial tribunals, Pliny indicates to Trajan that he has arranged to have these particular Christians sent to Rome.[14]

3. PLINY'S PROCEDURES FOR APOSTATES

Especially because they serve to accentuate the faithfulness of those who persevered in the faith, Pliny's reports to Trajan regarding a number of apostate Christians should be considered at least briefly. From the standpoint of a sociology of a religious movement under political pressure, the lines that Pliny penned in section six of his letter are especially significant. For memorably, this section adverts to the role played by an informer, indicates that some of those denounced had apostasized two to twenty (!) years previously, and suggests that some of those brought to Pliny admitted to being Christians at one time but then distanced themselves from any (recent) Christian commitment:

Others whose names were given to me by an informer, first admitted the charge and then denied it; they said that they had ceased to be Christians two or more years previously, and some of them even twenty years ago. They all did reverence to your statue and the images of the gods in the same way as the others, and reviled the name of Christ (*Letters* X.96,6).

Also to be noted in this passage is Pliny's report that he employed a two-part test in an effort to establish that those claiming to be apostates truly were such. The first part of this test, that concerning reverence to the Roman gods and to Trajan's statue, has already been mentioned in the preceding chapter where it was argued that such a procedure might well have originated with Domitian.[15] Thus the second part of the test, that regarding the cursing of Christ, remains to be considered here.

To curse Christ; to revile the name and the person of Christ. Pliny had been told by his informer that no *true* Christian would ever do such a thing just as no true Christian would ever beseech the Roman gods and offer wine and incense to the emperor's statue.[16] And surely in at least these aspects his informer supplied him with correct information.

It is perhaps worth reflecting here for just a moment on the contrast between the persevering and the apostasizing Christians as they respectively stood before Pliny and responded to his questions and initiatives. For those in the former group, confessing the name of Christ was everything. They would do so in response to each of Pliny's questions, knowing full well that death would be the outcome after they did so for the third time. For those in the latter group, the name of Christ was nothing or at least very little. It had mattered to them in the past, for they had formerly sought to be counted among those called Christians. But now, whatever their circumstances in the intervening time period, it was possible for them, either in strength or in weakness, to curse the name they formerly had professed.

Their act of cursing Christ, along with their performance of the other parts of Pliny's test, was seemingly the means by which these former Christians preserved their lives. True, Pliny does not explicitly report to Trajan that his practice had been to release apostate Christians now willing to make these faithless gestures. However, in another section of his letter he states that he has released those who denied ever having been Christian once they had buttressed their denials by performing these two tests.[17] And, when he summarizes the situation at the end of the letter, Pliny claims that his measures have resulted in some successes against the Christian movement. He refers to the fact that there has been an upsurge in worship at the pagan temples. What may well be implied is that those who apostasized were pardoned and released with the proviso that they participate in pagan worship and/or purchase the sacrificial meats used in such worship.[18] Indeed, the final sentence of his letter seems designed to persuade Trajan that a pardon is a highly effective response to give to those who renounce their Christianity. Indeed, more Christians might be "reformed," in other words, might renounce their faith, if they knew that by doing so they were sure to obtain a pardon:

> It is easy to infer from this that a great many people could be reformed if they were given an opportunity to repent (*Letters* X.96,10).

Structurally, Pliny's question about pardon for the apostates could be positioned in the next section where some of his other questions will be treated. However, thematically it is advisable to note in the present context that Pliny is less than certain about his own course in the matter of the apostates and desires a directive from Trajan. As just argued, Pliny seems to have been inclined toward a lenient approach in dealing with the apostates. However, his way of phrasing his question to Trajan shows that he envisions the possibility that the emperor himself may advocate a more severe course. Pliny frames his question to cover two important aspects. With one stroke he asks whether those who renounce their belief shall be granted a pardon. With a return stroke he asks whether they should still undergo punishment for their past involvement even though they now repudiate their former position.

In his reply Trajan is quite clear as to the course of action he wishes to have followed. He affirms the more lenient approach. The first sentence of his rescript indicates his overall approval for the approach that Pliny has followed, and he subsequently comments favorably on the particular case of the apostates. Since more will be said below concerning his decision in the case of those who persevered as Christians, those lines of the letter are omitted from consideration at this juncture.

Also to be noted in the passage that now follows is the fact that Trajan states clearly that Pliny shall not consider how strongly committed these Christians were in the past (" . . . however suspect his past conduct may be.") as long as they give a definite sign of having repented. Finally, note that Trajan only makes mention of one of Pliny's tests for determining apostasy:

> You have followed the right course of procedure, my dear Pliny, in your examination of the cases of persons charged with being Christians. . . . But in the case of anyone who denies that he is a Christian and makes it clear that he is not by offering prayers to our gods, he is to be pardoned as a result of his repentance however suspect his past conduct may be (*Letters* X.97).

4. PLINY'S SPECIFIC QUESTIONS TO TRAJAN

Before analyzing the specific subject areas in which Pliny solicits Trajan's decisions, it must be emphasized that Pliny himself has already concluded that Christians have not been guilty of criminal behavior *apart from the fact that they profess Christianity*. As noted above, he reached this conclusion as a result of his interrogation of the apostates and his torture of two Christian women. Seemingly, his insight on this point has been a principal factor in his decision to suspend the trials until he can gain Trajan's perspective on the matter.

From the standpoint of the present study, Pliny's requests to Trajan can be categorized as one major and three minor questions. One of these minor questions, whether apostates should be punished for having been Christians in the first place, has already been dealt with above. The way is thus now open for a consideration of what Pliny asks concerning the crime of per-severing Christians, concerning appropriate punishment, and concerning the procedures by which they are brought to trial.

Pliny's question regarding the offense of Christians is, of course, the question that is of major import within the present study. Pointedly, Pliny asks Trajan whether it is "the name itself" (*nomen ipsum*) that is punish-able. Or is it the criminal conduct associated with the name that is really the object of punishment? Conceivably, by framing the question in this fashion, Pliny may have been subtly raising the possibility that the fact of Christian commitment might not be a punishable offense. He still refers to Christianity as a "degenerate cult" (*superstitionem pravam*).[19] Nevertheless, he has concluded from his questioning of the apostates and his interroga-tion, by torture, of two Christian women that Christianity's social practices are essentially harmless.

Still, Pliny clearly does reckon with the possibility that Trajan will want Christians punished "because of the name." And accordingly, he also asks direction regarding the type of punishment that is appropriate. This inquiry may be regarded as minor inasmuch as it assumes importance only in the instance of an affirmative reply to his first question. Once again a certain leaning toward mildness may be present in the way in which Pliny poses the issue. Given the data he provides it is not possible to know whether he has already been taking the qualifying factor of age into account when he has punished persevering Christians—he simply reports that, when they persevere after his third question, he orders their execution. Yet clearly he adverts to this factor in placing the matter before Trajan: "Nor am I at all sure whether any distinction should be made between them on the grounds of age, or if young people and adults should be treated alike" (*Letters* X.96,2).

After commenting to Trajan that he had not previously been present at the trials of Christians and then explaining his general ignorance about the matter of punishment, Pliny also mentions that he is not informed regarding " . . . the grounds for starting an investigation and how far it should be pressed" (*Letters* X.96,2). He thus solicits Trajan's guidance in this area as well. It later becomes clear that he himself was subsequently influenced by the above mentioned anonymous pamphlet and seemingly proceeded to arrest all whose names were listed. In addition, as mentioned, he also relied upon an informer for further information regarding suspected Christians.

Taken together these various concerns may be said to constitute Pliny's final question to Trajan. Essentially it is a question about the procedures that can be used in identifying Christians and bringing them to trial. And like his two other "minor" questions, it is a question that will not have practical significance if Trajan's response should be that Christians will no longer be punished at all.

5. THE FORCE OF TRAJAN'S REPLY

Such was not to be the reality of Trajan's reply. In contrast with his legate's long, explanation-filled letter of some sixty-one lines, Trajan's rescript is remarkably brief, running only to eleven lines. Without going into detail on any of Pliny's questions, Trajan's reply provides definite answers on two of the minor questions and, by implication, on the third as well. It is, of course, his exacting reply to Pliny's lead question that possesses primary importance.

Without using the term used by Pliny, *nomen ipsum* ("the name itself"), Trajan does make it clear that Christians who persevere in professing the name of Christ are to be dealt with harshly. His terse comment on this point is as follows: "If they are brought before you and the charge against them is proved, *they must be punished*" (*Letters* X.97; italics added). Unmistakably and momentously Trajan is thus commending the execution Christians who persevere in their faith.

With his rescript so worded, Trajan thus clearly rejects Pliny's suggestion that Christians not be liable for punishment simply on the grounds that they are Christians. In Trajan's view, which now becomes the supremely authoritative view, other crimes do not have to be established. Christians, because they are Christians, are now definitively liable to the sentence of death.[20]

It is impossible to say exactly what factors influenced Trajan to take such a position. What other sources of information, if any, did he have regarding Christians? At this juncture it should be recalled that Pliny's letter seemingly implied that Trajan had some awareness of earlier trials involving Christians. However, in this instance, the rescript provides no explanation for the decision taken.[21] From the standpoint of committed Christians in the province of Bithynia-Pontus, Trajan's decision was a harsh one indeed. The fundamental severity of his reply must not be overlooked even though his responses to Pliny's other questions are considerably more moderate.

The moderate character of some aspects of his reply is nowhere more evident than in the lines penned in response to Pliny's question about correct procedures. In writing that "these people must not be hunted out . . . " and by stating that " . . . pamphlets circulated anonymously must play no part in any accusation," Trajan actually corrects Pliny's practices in these two areas. But again, such "enlightened" policy prescriptions have an ironic dimension given Trajan's foregoing decision that the profession of Christian faith should be regarded as a capital offense. This aspect of irony is further enhanced by the statement with which Trajan chooses to conclude his rescript. In stating his decision that anonymous pamphlets should have no place in the proceedings, the emperor reflects about the requirements of an enlightened age: "They [the anonymous pamphlets] create the worst sort of precedent and are quite out of keeping with the spirit of our age" (*Letters* X.97).

As indicated above, with respect to those Christians who apostasized, Trajan's rescript confirmed Pliny's view that those apostate Christians who indicated their "repentance" by performing certain tests should be pardoned.[22] Thus the only one of Pliny's questions not yet considered regards whether the punishment meted out to persevering Christians should take account of such factors as age. Here Trajan's response is indirect. The only statement within the rescript that borders on addressing this subject is the statement, " ... for it is impossible to lay down a general rule to a fixed formula." However, given the context this reflection may apply as much to the means of testing that Pliny has devised as it does to the matter of the degree of punishment.

The overall force of Trajan's response is thus not to give his legate any specific direction on the subject of punishment but rather to leave the matter to Pliny's discretion. Indeed, such an outcome, the (indirect) affirmation of the provincial governor's discretion for taking relevant factors into account when sentencing, would not be unusual within the Roman framework.[23] Trajan knows that Pliny has heretofore been executing persevering Christians, and he officially authorizes and commends this practice. However, Trajan does not determine whether or to what degree Pliny should take account of other qualifying factors when he passes sentence.

6. IMPLICATIONS FOR BITHYNIA-PONTUS AND ADJACENT PROVINCES

Before moving to chapter four and an analysis of the text of John's Gospel, it is appropriate to summarize the consequences that Trajan's reply presumably had for Pliny in Bithynia-Pontus and to discuss briefly its implications for governors and other officials in the other provinces of the empire. Had Pliny but taken time to write out his reactions and his responses once he had received Trajan's rescript, the present task of interpretation would be considerably easier.

Proceeding in light of Trajan's directives, Pliny presumably would no longer react to anonymous pamphlets but would rather wait until the opponents of Christians appeared personally before him for the purpose of denouncing them. Then, to determine the truth of the matter, Pliny would have had the suspected Christians brought before him and, after warning them about the punishment awaiting them, would have asked them three times if they were Christians. If after the third time they persisted in their commitment, then they normally would be handed over for execution, with the possibility that more lenient punishment might be used for those who were younger, and so forth.

If some of those so denounced should deny to Pliny that they were now or ever had been Christians, he would then presumably conduct certain tests to confirm the truth of their statement. Previously he had asked them to invoke the Roman gods, to offer wine and incense before the statue of Trajan, and to curse Christ. Presumably he would continue to employ these same three tests reasoning that, although Trajan had only expressly mentioned the first test, he certainly did not prohibit the other two.

If his own views were along the lines described in section three above, Pliny may personally have had misgivings about the harsh measures toward committed Christians that the rescript indicated. Nevertheless, loyal even to the excess of according Trajan more than human standing, Pliny would certainly have carried the emperor's decisions out faithfully.

With respect to the consequences of Trajan's rescript for Bithynia-Pontus under Pliny's successors and for the other provinces of the empire, the situation is less than clear.[24] For one thing, the available evidence indicates that a rescript directed to a particular province did not have the force of an empire-wide law. Nevertheless, it is hard to imagine that the governors of other provinces, particularly those adjacent to Bithynia-Pontus, would not regard the points of the rescript as useful guideposts in dealing with any problems involving Christians within their own provinces. And above all, it must not be minimized that Trajan had now personally reached and stated the conclusion that Christians were inimical enough to be eradicated—if they were denounced as Christians.

It is thus the case that all of these factors—those that are certain, those that are probable, those that are possible—need to be kept in mind in trying to form some construction of the situation of Christians in the Eastern provinces of the Roman empire during the Flavio-Trajanic period. One final point not to be overlooked is that by Pliny's own assessment the Christian movement—"this wretched cult"—was numerically significant in Bithynia-Pontus by this time. Socially inclusive, it was also geographically well dispersed:

> For a great many individuals of every age and class, both men and women, are being brought to trial, and this is likely to continue. It is not only the towns, but villages and rural districts too which are infected through contact with this wretched cult (*Letters* X.96,9).

4

The Sovereignty of Jesus

As a consequence of the analysis made in chapters two and three an appreciation has now been gained for several detrimental practices and patterns that existed in the Roman empire in the latter half of the first century. As indicated, from the time of Nero, and even previously, claims antithetical to Christians were being advanced by and on behalf of those ascending to the imperial throne. Second, from the time of Vespasian onward, the collection of the Jewish Tax was a practice that had the potential for engendering the denunciation of both Christians and Jews. Third, from the era of Trajan and very probably from the reign of Domitian, official trials involving Christians were held, trials in which the "crime" of remaining a Christian was punishable by death.

In terms of the present study's principal thrusts, the exalted claims of the various emperors and the actual trials and executions of Christians are of primary interest. Nevertheless, the material presented in reference to the Jewish Tax should not be neglected. For reflections about the administration of this tax and its potential for impacting Christians as well as Jews can contribute to a heightened sense of imagination about the relation of both groups to the Roman state during this period. It is thus the case that the interactions of Christians with Roman rule were not restricted to limit situations in which Christ's disciples were face to face with Roman claims and practices that were fundamentally intolerable to them.

The text of the Fourth Gospel now appropriately moves to the center stage within this study. However, before beginning this part of the analysis, a brief word regarding methodology and confirmation is in order. It is especially important that such aspects be discussed now in order that readers may have appropriate expectations regarding the kinds of conclusions that can be reached when John's text is analyzed in the light of these Roman factors.

1. METHODOLOGY AND CONFIRMATION

As a prelude to a discussion of the methodology governing the present study, it is useful to review the broadly phrased thesis stated at the begin-

27

ning of chapter one: "In depicting Jesus' identity and mission within his Gospel, the evangelist John was concerned to present elements and themes that were especially significant for Christian readers facing Roman imperial claims and for any who faced Roman persecution."

While the general wording of this thesis was initially helpful for indicating the basic thrust of the present study, it is now appropriate to specify that there are actually two closely related assertions intended within this summary sentence. The first assertion has to do with the text of the Gospel. It is that elements and themes present with the text of John's Gospel respond extremely well to the situation of Christians facing Roman claims and any who faced Roman persecution. The second assertion concerns the mind of John. It is that, in depicting Jesus' identity and mission within his Gospel, John *consciously chose* to include and even to emphasize particular elements and themes.

While these two assertions are distinct, there are two common features to the methodology by which both of them are appropriately addressed. In both cases external data for confirming conclusively the validity of the assertion are lacking to such a point that the assertion cannot be established from external evidence alone. Secondly, in both cases the character of the riches contained within John's final text *is* sufficient to justify the assertion.

What does it mean to say that external empirical data are not available for establishing conclusively either assertion? In general it means that written or archaeological data comparable to that cited in the analysis of the Jewish Tax in chapter two are lacking in these instances.

Thus, with respect to the first assertion, there is no presently available testimony by any Roman or Christian author that early Christians actually utilized the Gospel of John to guide them and strengthen them in the face of imperial claims and/or persecution. Nor have any archaeological artifacts yet been unearthed in which Roman trial documents portray Christians citing John's text in making their defenses before Roman governors.

Similarly, with respect to the second assertion, no surviving work from any early Christian writer states that the intention to strengthen Christians beleaguered by the claims and persecutions of Roman officials was one of John's definite purposes in publishing his Gospel. Nor, archaeologically speaking, has there ever been any discovery relating to John and those around him comparable to the discoveries at Qumran for the first-century Jewish group, the Essenes.

If the two assertions contained in the thesis of this study are thus not susceptible to external confirmation, what then is the methodology to be adopted? As indicated above it is a methodology that primarily utilizes the text of the Gospel itself. In terms of the first assertion, the primary procedure is to demonstrate a convincingly high degree of correlation between elements and themes of the text and the fundamental circumstances of the first-century Christians under Roman rule. For the second assertion, the basic procedure is to advert to the precise way in which these elements are present within John's account, arguing in particular that the character of John's concluding chapters indicates that he was personally conscious of these elements and themes.

Certainly this brief description is not sufficient to resolve every concern relative to methodology. However, the alternative to embarking upon a fuller explanation of this approach is actually to implement it. And thus on the assumption that this methodology will be grasped more readily once concrete results are obtained from utilizing it, it is now appropriate to embark on the analysis of John's text itself.

One final note concerns the pattern of the analysis to be made in the next section of this chapter and that to be made in the following chapters of this study. In order to orient themselves to the way in which John's text will be related to its Roman context readers may well wish to note carefully sections 6.1, 6.3, and 7.4 within the following chapters. It is in these sections that efforts will be made to indicate the high relevance of John's account for Christians challenged by Roman imperial claims and Christians under the threat of Roman persecution.

In effect then, the pattern of chapters four through seven is as follows: (a) an overview of Jesus' ministry and an analysis of his Roman trial followed by reflections of the meaning of this content for John's readers; (b) analysis of Jesus' farewell discourses followed by reflections as to the power of these discourses when read within a setting of Roman intimidation; and (c) analysis of the risen Jesus' interactions with his disciples, again followed by reflections concerning the impact of these passages. Chapter eight will conclude this study by focusing upon John's purposes in writing.

2. AN OVERVIEW OF JESUS' SOVEREIGN STATUS

It is hardly an exaggeration to say that the entire Gospel of John is permeated with the sovereignty of Jesus. Jesus possesses sovereign standing from the first moment that he is present within John's Gospel. He manifests his sovereignty in the signs that he performs and asserts it in numerous instances within his discourses. His strategic actions until the time of his hour also attest to his sovereign powers. He remains sovereign in the circumstances of his arrest, trial, and death. His sovereignty is then confirmed and manifested by a series of post-resurrection appearances to his disciples.

To those familiar with the prevailing categories of Johannine scholarship, it will be apparent from the foregoing statements that the concept of sovereignty being delineated here is closely related to the widely recognized concept of John's high christology.[1] However, now to be elaborated is the insight that John's indication of Jesus' exalted status also functions to affirm Jesus' sovereignty in the face of competing claims of sovereignty made by various Roman officials.

Regardless of whether the first eighteen verses of the Fourth Gospel were composed separately, they were very definitely positioned as an introduction to the remainder of the Gospel at the time when John readied the Gospel for circulation. And thus it is well to begin the analysis of sovereignty with a brief consideration of several of the prologue's affirmations, even though the entire eighteen verses cannot be systematically treated. What essentially does the prologue state about Jesus? That he is the Word made flesh (1:14), the Word, who was *with God* in the beginning and who *was God* (1:1).[2]

The full implications of these affirmations for those who would be Jesus' disciples will be developed more fully as the Gospel proceeds. Yet within a situation in which allegiance to Jesus is presumably at issue, what a summoning assertion of faith for John to begin with. And as the prologue continues John makes clear that this Word of God who is Jesus has been entrusted with a mission on behalf of God, a mission involving light and life for all who would believe in him.

Even at this point the assertion that the themes of the prologue provide, as one of their dimensions of meaning, a strong affirmation of Jesus' unsurpassed standing is easily grasped. But simply to reinforce the point that so many verses of the prologue section contribute to this idea, verse 1:18 is appropriately considered.[3] There John states, "No one has ever seen God; the only Son, who is in the bosom of the Father, he has made him known." Particularly rich in terms of what it mediates to John's readers, it should be noted that this verse functions in two directions. On the one hand, it affirms the Son's (Jesus') privileged position as the revealer of the Father; on the other hand, it stresses that *no one else* has ever *seen* God.

In moving from the prologue to a consideration of John's descriptions of Jesus' public ministry, several factors must be kept in mind with respect to the nature of John's presentation. John's Gospel concentrates intensely upon Jesus' origin, his identity, and his mission; and it characteristically expresses and re-expresses a number of important truths through various literary forms. As a consequence, in embarking upon John's Gospel, readers find a related series[4] of dialogues, discourses, and signs—all having to do with Jesus' identity and all integrated within a carefully presented narrative of Jesus' movements to and from Jerusalem.[5]

From the standpoint of the present study, it is possible to regard John's chapters treating Jesus' public ministry as having a certain "logic regarding sovereignty" about them. It must be emphasized that there is much more occurring within these chapters than can be categorized adequately under the heading of sovereignty. There is, for example, much that concerns belief in, and the gradations of belief in, Jesus.[6] Still, in the final analysis the presence of other content themes does not preclude the interpretation that sovereignty is present in Jesus' dialogues and discourses, that sovereignty is confirmed through his signs, and that sovereignty is manifested in his strategic maneuvers.

Even in terms of the dialogues and discourses that John presents Jesus engaging in and delivering, it must again be cautioned that there is an abundance of nuances and subtleties that cannot be adverted to here. (Indeed, at this point, readers of the present study may wish to pause for a reflective reading of the dialogues, discourses, and other elements contained in chapters 2 through 11 of John's Gospel.) However, what can be asserted is that the dialogues and discourses that are so carefully delineated in the first half of John's Gospel almost all function to show Jesus making various assertions and claims on behalf of his own sovereign standing.

The well-studied phenomenon of Jesus' claims to be "the Son" and the equally well-studied phenomenon of his assertions using the words "I am" may both be mentioned as examples of how Jesus' sovereignty is portrayed by John. Multifaceted indeed and rich in subtle shades of meaning are the many statements that the Johannine Jesus makes utilizing each of these terms. Jesus *as Son*[7] claims to have been sent by the Father out of love for the world. He is descended from the heavenly realm and will return there upon the completion of his mission. He is obedient to the Father and yet is so closely identified with the Father that to hear and to respond to Jesus is to hear and respond to the Father. He has the Father's authority to judge all things. And those who believe in him gain eternal life while those who refuse to believe perish.

Similar, perhaps even more dramatic claims to sovereign status are also present in the passages in which John portrays Jesus using the "I am" (*egō eimi*) construction.[8] When the Johannine Jesus uses these words absolutely it seems unassailable that he is placing himself on the level of God and claiming to speak as with the authority of God.[9]

In describing the public ministry of Jesus, John does not describe Jesus working "miracles" but rather as performing seven momentous "signs."[10] Three of these signs featured healings: the healing of the royal official's son at Cana (4:43-54), the healing of the crippled man in Jerusalem (5:1-44), and the healing of the blind man, also in Jerusalem (9:1-41). Three of these signs entailed sublating the laws of nature: changing the water to wine at Cana (2:1-11), the multiplication of loaves at the edge of the Sea of Galilee (6:1-15), and Jesus' subsequent walking upon the water of the Sea of Galilee (6:16-21). And the seventh sign, in several respects the culmination of the series, is constituted by Jesus' restoration of Lazarus to life (11:1-57).

Once again, an important aspect to be noted regarding these passages is that each of these signs is highly christological in its character and, from the standpoint of this study, each makes a significant contribution to the theme of Jesus' sovereign status. Viewing them together, the signs may in fact be regarded as logically buttressing the claim to exalted standing that Jesus makes in his discourses and dialogues. John's Jesus is indeed sovereign over diseases and over the laws of nature. Even more significantly, he is sovereign over death.

This latter aspect, sovereignty in terms of life and death, is perhaps worth dwelling upon for a moment. Jesus adverts to the subject of life and death within his dialogues and discourses, and as just noted, his raising of Lazarus dramatically confirmed his powers in this area. The point, then, is that there are consequences to Jesus' sovereign status. It is not simply that Jesus calls people to believe in him because of assertions concerning his origin, his identity, and his mission. Over and beyond this, he calls them to belief because this belief is a matter of their life and death.[11]

Finally, it is to be noted that John's narrative also illuminates Jesus' sovereignty by depicting him as possessing a supra-human knowledge regarding various aspects of his situation and as possessing an innate ability for circumventing the machinations of his opponents. In different ways both of these aspects of John's portrayal advance the understanding that Jesus' sovereignty is not such as to be affected by the hostile intentions and maneuvers of his opponents.

As illustrative of Jesus' overarching knowledge concerning the interior motives of human beings and concerning the course of his own ministry, three passages may be cited.[12] In the first, 2:24-25, John makes the stunning statement that Jesus did not need to have anyone inform him about human behavior because he knew all human beings and knew what was inside them. The other two passages both contain the assertion that Jesus had foreknowledge concerning his betrayal. In verse 6:64 John indicates that Jesus knew those who did not believe and knew specifically who would betray him.[13] Significantly, this verse also indicates that Jesus had knowledge of these things from the outset. In 13:18-19 Jesus gives a still further indication of his knowledge concerning his imminent betrayal. Wanting to reassure his faithful disciples lest they be scandalized in the event, he first states clearly that not all of them would be faithful. Then a few verses later, he identifies Judas as the actual betrayer (13:26).

Generalizing with respect to the subject of Jesus' strategic behavior, a useful summarizing statement is to say that Jesus outmaneuvers his opponents with remarkable dexterity and then remains sovereignly beyond their reach until his hour[14] is finally at hand. The following chapter of this study will consider briefly the various persons and entities who are Jesus' adversaries and some of their efforts against him. It suffices to observe in this context that Jesus successfully utilizes various tactics against them.[15]

For example, in several instances John uses forms of *kryptō*, the Greek word often translated as "secret" or "hidden" or preferably as "cryptic" in describing Jesus' movements and maneuvers. Somewhat startlingly, John's first use of this word occurs when he reports in 7:4 that Jesus' "brothers" challenged him to go up to the feast in Jerusalem on the grounds that he had too much been working "in secret." John then portrays Jesus telling his brothers that he will not go up for the feast (7:8). However, Jesus changes plans and goes up to the feast, but "in secret" (7:10). It is interesting to speculate regarding the visual image that John intended to convey in giving this report, in other words, regarding the image evoked by the words that Jesus moved secretly and then appeared dramatically in the temple when the feast was half over.

Within chapters 7, 8 and 9, Jesus' movements and his maneuvers vis à vis his opponents are remarkable. Jesus appears, controverts, escapes arrest (7:30), reappears, proclaims, escapes arrest (7:44), reappears, controverts, escapes stoning (8:59), performs the sign of healing the blind man, and escapes stoning and arrest even though his adversaries literally have stones in their hands during this last episode (10:31,39).

Then Jesus strategically departs Jerusalem for the territory across the Jordan only to return to Bethany (the raising of Lazarus). He then leaves for Ephraim[16] only to return dramatically to Jerusalem. Yet even then, with the time of his "hour" at hand, John portrays him once more leaving the crowds of the city, secreting himself (*ekrybē*) from them (12:36b).

Jesus' unpredictable, mysterious, cryptic movements are of more than passing significance within the more general portrayal of Jesus' sovereignty that John sets before his readers. This feature of Jesus' sovereignty is further underscored by the confusion and disorder that John attributes to Jesus' opponents throughout these chapters. For at different times in the proceedings, they either simply do not know where he is (7:11), think that he might be intending to go to the Diaspora (7:35-36), or are perplexed over whether he will once again come to Jerusalem (11:55-56; 12:19). More will be said about Jesus' opponents and their efforts against him in the following chapter of this work. What is clear at this point is that they are never successful in apprehending him (either through verbal attack or through physical and lethal attacks) until the time of his "hour." And even then, as will be seen, Jesus still remains sovereign in the midst of the legal and extra-legal proceedings against him.

Summarizing, the opening chapters of John's Gospel testify to the surpassing sovereignty of Jesus in a multiplicity of ways.[17] John himself adverts to Jesus' sovereign standing in the memorable verses of his prologue and then presents a narrative concerning Jesus' public ministry in which Jesus' dialogues and discourses and his signs and strategic conduct all bespeak one whose standing is "from above." Indeed, it is on the basis of his exalted sovereign standing that Jesus invites those who encounter him to the response of belief, belief in him and in all that he reveals concerning the Father's purposes.

3. THREE TITLES OF ACCLAIM

Within his finished Gospel John portrays various gradations of belief as he describes the ways in which different persons and groups responded to Jesus. In the section that now follows, the affirmation of Jesus as "Savior of the World" by the townspeople of Samaria will be considered, and so will Thomas' famous confession of Jesus as "my Lord and my God." In addition, the use of the title "Lord" by Mary, Martha, Mary Magdalene, and others in their respective responses to Jesus will also be analyzed. Inasmuch as these three terms are the very ones described in chapter two above as having been bestowed upon various Roman emperors, the presence of these titles within John's finished account must be regarded as extraordinarily significant.

A. Savior of the World

John's presentation of the episodes in Samaria, which culminate in Jesus' being acclaimed as Savior of the world, is a remarkable presentation indeed. However, before giving specific attention to those episodes it should be noted that the image of Jesus as *saving the world* is not limited to the Samaritans' acclamation of him as Savior but is also extensively portrayed in other sections of the Gospel. In his dialogue with Nicodemus (3:17) and within his farewell discourse (12:44) Jesus himself describes his mission as involving a "saving" of the world. In addition, this image is present in a number of other passages (1:29; 3:16-17; 6:33; 6:51).

It is important that these foregoing instances be kept as a frame of reference for the issue that will emerge at the end of the present discussion, namely, the issue of whether "Savior of the world" as a title should be understood as restricted solely to Jesus. Nevertheless, that issue as well as other points of interpretation can only be properly addressed after the Samaritan woman's wonderful progression in understanding different aspects of Jesus' identity is first appreciated. For as John describes her encounter with Jesus (4:7-26), there is a remarkable development in her own understanding of who he actually is.

The woman begins with the recognition that Jesus is a Jew (4:9). Then as the dialogue with Jesus continues and as he leads her forward by his responses she sees him as someone perhaps greater than Jacob (4:12), as a prophet (4:19), and as the Messiah (4:25,29). Indeed, she gradually becomes so convinced of his exalted identity that she eventually proclaims him to her townspeople (4:28-29).

John then portrays these other Samaritans as being so impressed and persuaded by the woman's testimony that they come out to Jesus and beseech him to *remain*[18] with them (4:40). The evangelist then supplies two further notes: (a) Jesus actually *remained* with them for two days, and (b) that because of Jesus' word during this time, even more of the townspeople came to believe in him.

It is then that John reports the Samaritans' culminating confession of Jesus. Note that in the sentences now cited the element of strong personal belief is a prelude to the dramatic confession then given:

> They said to the woman, "It is no longer because of your words that we believe, for we have heard for ourselves, and we know that this is indeed *the Savior of the world*" (4:42; italics added).

What then are the dimensions of meaning attached to this title as it now stands within John's account? The first observation to be made is that, as used within this context, "Savior of the world" connotes an extremely high level of sovereignty. This observation follows from the fact that the title is bestowed at the conclusion of Jesus' encounter with the Samaritans, an encounter in which several other significant titles have already been bestowed upon him. "Savior of the world" in effect tends to gather the aspects of meaning associated with such previous titles as "prophet" and "messiah" and indicates that Jesus' real identity is still greater.[19] The title itself states that Jesus is Savior, not of any particular people but rather of the entire world. Significantly this acclaim is given to him, a Jew, by townspeople who are Samaritans. It is nevertheless clear that the saving work being attributed to him extends far beyond the territories of Judea and Samaria and Galilee.[20]

But is it John's sense in presenting this entire episode that Jesus *alone* is Savior of the world? Does John understand the Samaritans' ringing acclamation belongs *only* to Jesus and not to any other person or entity. There are factors within the passage itself and within the larger framework of the Gospel to suggest that these questions should be answered affirmatively. Certainly the most immediately obvious factor is the presence of the word "indeed" (*alēthōs*) within the Samaritans' concluding confession: ". . . this is *indeed* the Savior of the world."

Other elements in the scene John portrays also contribute to the impression that it is a confession given restrictively to Jesus. The townspeople have arrived at such a point of conviction after Jesus has *remained* with them for a period of two days. And thus their avowal to the woman that, over and beyond her words encouraging them to believe, " . . . we have heard for ourselves, and we know." In this statement every pronoun, phrase, and clause indicates that the Samaritans' solemn judgment about Jesus' identity has not been spoken casually.

To sharpen the point that is at issue here, it may be asked whether this particular passage or John's Gospel as a whole is open to the interpretation that other persons or entities other than Jesus can rightly be regarded as "Savior of the world." In other words, is the emphasis upon Jesus' saving power here and in the Gospel as a whole such as to preclude that an emperor such as Nero or a pagan god of healing might also appropriately be given such acclaim?[21]

At this juncture attention should be given to the paragraphs opening this section in which reference was made to the other Gospel passages attesting to Jesus' work and mission in saving the world. Who else *truly* has such a work? Patently it is absurd to hold that within the perspective of John's Gospel such a title could also be attributed to any god or mythic force. And surely it cannot be conceived that the Gospel of John attributes any *real* role in the "saving" of the world to the power of a Roman emperor.[22]

B. Lord

Within the Gospel of John, "Lord" (*kyrios*) is the preeminent title of address used by those who truly believe in Jesus. This pattern holds for the time of Jesus' public ministry and also characterizes the interval of his post-resurrection appearances.[23] In addition, after Jesus' resurrection, Mary Magdalene, the beloved disciple, and others use the term "the Lord" (*ho kyrios*) in speaking of Jesus objectively.

In addition to these types of uses by disciples, "Lord" is also used by a number of other persons within the Gospel who are in the process of coming to belief in Jesus.[24] This is particularly true for those involved in situations in which Jesus heals.[25] In addition, John himself as narrator occasionally uses "Lord" in reference to Jesus. And finally, when he washed his disciples' feet, Jesus himself explicitly accepted this term in self-designation:[26]

> You call me Teacher and Lord; and you are right for so I am. If I then, your Lord and Teacher, have washed your feet . . . (13:13-14a).

From the standpoint of the present study what is particularly significant in respect to many of these occurrences of "Lord" is that they serve unmistakably to convey and enhance the meaning that Jesus is a figure of exalted standing, someone whose sovereign power extends even to the limits of death and life. In order to illustrate this point, an analysis will now be made of the use of this title in three settings: (a) as it is used in Martha and Mary's interactions with Jesus at the time of Lazarus' death, (b) as it is used in the post-resurrection appearances of chapter 21, and (c) as it is used within the resurrection and post-resurrection scenes of chapter 20. This last study will, in turn, prepare the way for an assessment of the acclamation "my Lord and my God" at the end of chapter 20.

Initially, when Martha and Mary seek out Jesus, Lazarus is seriously ill. In contacting him they address him as "Lord" and their message also evidences their trust that Jesus has the power to restore Lazarus to health (11:3-4). By the time Jesus arrives on the scene, Lazarus has died. However, Martha (again addressing Jesus as "Lord") expresses a trust that even now Jesus can intervene with power (11:21-22). In a beautiful exchange Jesus asserts that he has sovereign power over death and asks Martha if she believes this (11:23-26). In her response Martha wonderfully expresses her belief in Jesus' exalted, sovereign standing: "Yes, *Lord*; I believe that you are the Christ, the Son of God, he who is coming into the world" (11:27; italics added).[27]

Before proceeding to the tomb, Jesus next meets with Mary, who like her sister, addresses him as "Lord" and with Martha's exact confession (11:32b). Arriving at the site, Jesus reassures Martha of his power to intervene and then prays aloud to the Father. Remarkably, he prays not in petition but rather for the purpose of indicating to those assembled his own close relationship with the Father (11:41b-42). Jesus, the one hailed and addressed as "Lord" throughout this episode, then authoritatively and sovereignly bids Lazarus to come forth from the tomb (11:43-44).

Considerably more will be said about the material contained in John 21 in chapter seven below. At that time, too, the grounds for considering the verses of that chapter as a legitimate resource for this study will also be explained. However, at the present state it suffices to consider briefly that "Lord" is the sole title by which Peter and the beloved disciple address or refer to Jesus within that chapter.

In this regard there are five occurrences to be noted. When the beloved disciple first recognizes the risen Jesus on the beach he exclaims to Peter, "It is the Lord" (21:7a). Subsequently, when Peter makes his threefold confession of love for Jesus, he addresses Jesus in each instance reverently as "Lord" (21:15,16,17). Finally, when Peter, the beloved disciple, and the risen Jesus are walking along the beach, Peter asks of Jesus, "Lord, what about this man?" (21:21).

Again, what is significant about this usage (especially when a similar pattern of usage is observed for John 20) is that Jesus, the one who has risen to a glorified state, Jesus, the one who is now sovereign beyond the limits of space and time, is consistently addressed and referred to as "Lord." This title is thus one used by his intimate disciples to express their sense of who he is and how he is to be named.

With respect to chapter 20, it can be said that, even apart from its culminating scene containing Thomas' unsurpassed acclamation of Jesus, this chapter attests remarkably to two other aspects of Jesus' identity as Lord. First, in a striking pattern Mary Magdalene and then Jesus' other disciples refer to him as "the Lord" (20:2,18,25). Second, Mary is also now shown to refer to Jesus with emphatic personal allegiance as "my Lord." For, in reply to the angels' question about her weeping, she states, "Because they have taken away *my* Lord and I do not know where they have laid him" (20:13b; italics added).

It is interesting to reflect for a moment upon these two forms of usage. In the first case there is a note of objectivity, a note of absoluteness, conferred by the article. Jesus is *the* Lord. In contrast, the second use stresses a subjective and personal entering into relationship with Jesus as sovereign. Here Jesus is for Mary *her* Lord. He is the sovereign one to whom she is personally committed by reason of her belief, allegiance, and love.

Clearly these two aspects are complementary. For it is one and the same Jesus who is at once *Mary's* Lord and *the* Lord. Parenthetically it should be noted that a somewhat comparable subjective aspect in Jesus' disciples relationship with *the* Father is also now adverted to. For with particularly poignant words Jesus asks Mary to share with his other disciples that ". . . I am ascending to my Father and *your* Father, to my God and *your* God" (20:17b; italics added).

C. Lord and God

Keeping in mind the foregoing considerations relative to the usage of "Lord," the way is now open to a consideration of the memorable "my Lord and my God" confession made by Thomas at the end of chapter 20. With respect to the setting in which Thomas' confession occurs, it should be noted that the risen Jesus' powers are clearly in evidence in the scene John portrays. Jesus has already appeared to his disciples passing freely through their locked door and now, one week later, with Thomas present, he appears in their midst in a similar fashion. Seemingly this very fact is sufficient to engender Thomas' response of belief. In addition, the risen Jesus also indicates to Thomas that he is fully aware of the unbelieving comment that Thomas has made to the other disciples.

Faced with this experience of Jesus now transformed and sovereign beyond the limits of space and time, what is Thomas' response? In the original Greek, Thomas' outcry consists of six words, *kyrios mou kai ho theos mou* (20:28). In English this confession is rendered powerfully as: "my Lord and my God!"

Upon a moment's reflection it is soon apparent that Thomas' words wonderfully affirm Jesus' majestic standing and at the same time express a now deeply held personal allegiance. In these aspects it is reminiscent of Mary Magdalene's use of "my Lord." Yet clearly Thomas' final words now express an even greater range and solemnity.

As it now stands within John's Gospel there are several important dimensions of meaning attendant to Thomas' confession, three of which can now be adverted to. First, Thomas' confession unmistakably conveys an unsurpassed christological meaning and thus serves as a fitting summit point a Gospel that is so manifestly concerned with Jesus' exalted status.[28] Thomas' acclamation is indeed reminiscent of John's prologue statements that Jesus *was with* God and *was* God. And thus John approaches the conclusion of his Gospel with an acclamation that attests to Jesus' divine standing in a way that is fully comparable to what he himself stated at the beginning.

Second, Thomas' words also have meaning in terms of the theme of belief. Reluctant to believe without a direct experience of the risen Jesus, Thomas' confession now indicates his complete and unqualified belief in Jesus. Yet as Jesus' words in response to him make clear, Thomas' faith is one that has been arrived at on the basis of seeing. And blessed even more are those who believe without seeing (20:29).

Third, of particular interest in the perspective of the present study is the fact that Thomas' confession expresses in the strongest possible way his personal allegiance to Jesus. This point has already been mentioned above but is deserving of further emphasis here. It is the double presence of the personal adjective, *my*, with the words of exalted identity, "Lord" and "God" which accomplish this effect. Jesus has surpassed objective status as the Lord and God of the universe.[29] However, he is more than that in relation to Thomas. For Thomas, in addition, Jesus, is indisputably *my* Lord and *my* God.

One final aspect to be noted in drawing this section and this chapter to a close is the fact that Thomas' words and the entire scene John is portraying at this point allow for the risen Jesus' continuing presence. Jesus' sovereign status is not to be limited to a day, a week, a year. Nor is there any limit expressed for Thomas' allegiance to him. For, just as Jesus is unendingly Lord and God, so must Thomas' confession of him be unending.

5

The Roman Trial of Jesus

What information about Jesus did John's readership already possess before John published his Gospel? Seemingly, whether they were newly oriented to the Christian faith or whether they had matured in their faith through many years, one feature of Jesus' story about which they would have been well informed was the fact that Jesus had been tried and executed by the Roman governor of Judea. And thus it is reasonable to presume that John's narrative concerning this aspect of Jesus' life would have possessed great moment for all of his readers and especially any of them who were themselves subject to trials by the Roman authorities.

What would such readers have learned from John's account of Jesus' Roman trial? What would they have learned from John's reports concerning the circumstances of Jesus' death? These questions are of primary interest within the present chapter. However, it must be recognized that John's descriptions of Jesus' interactions with Pilate are embedded within a complexly woven narrative fabric in which Jesus' principal opponents also interact with Pilate and press for Jesus' destruction. And therefore considerations about Jesus' adversaries and their maneuvers against him appropriately precede an analysis of the significant exchanges that occur between Pilate and Jesus.

1. JESUS' OPPONENTS IN THE FOURTH GOSPEL

Who are Jesus' opponents acccording to John? And what is the nature of his conflict with them? To frame these questions and to seek answers for them involves coming to terms with the Fourth Gospel on various levels and engenders a profound respect for the subtleties and nuances of the account that John has provided.[1]

John depicts the following individuals, groups, and entities as exhibiting hostility toward Jesus: the Pharisees, the chief priests, Annas, Caiaphas, the authorities, the Jews,[2] the Council (Sanhedrin), Judas, Satan, and the world. Yet in essence, once John's complex use of the term "the Jews" is properly appreciated, the way is paved for the understanding that all of the just mentioned persons and entities essentially constitute a single allied group that willfully rejects Jesus' identity and consciously seeks his demise.[3]

Significantly, a close analysis of the occurrences of "the Jews" within John's narrative establishes that, when John uses this term *with negative connotation*, the reference is either to the chief priests or to the Pharisees or to both of these groups simultaneously.[4] In addition it can be shown that, when John uses the term "the authorities," the chief priests are again the group referred to.[5] Finally, it can also be demonstrated that John regards this alliance of the chief priests and the Pharisees as having been influenced by "the ruler of this world," who is Satan.[6]

The foregoing insights have particular importance with regard to the interpretation of John's account of Jesus' trial. It signifies that, for John, those pressing for Jesus' death are essentially an adversarial group comprised of chief priests and Pharisees. Clearly this also is an insight that carries major implications with respect to the tragic phenomenon of anti-Semitism within subsequent Christian tradition. Mistakenly, these Johannine references to "the Jews" have again and again been taken to signify opposition to Jesus by all Jews.

To emphasize this important point by restating it, the group pressuring Pilate for Jesus' death is essentially an alliance of chief priests and Pharisees and is distinct from the Jewish populace of Jerusalem. Their dispute with Jesus extends well back into the body of the Gospel, and fundamentally their hostility has been engendered by Jesus' exalted status and the claims he advances. The Roman authorities themselves are not mentioned until relatively late in the Gospel. However, once the Roman governor enters upon John's stage, he too becomes embroiled in the controversy about Jesus' identity. From beginning to end John's Gospel is essentially christological. In a very real sense Jesus comes to be tried before the Roman governor because he insists upon his own exalted identity and sharply attacks the Pharisees and the chief priests ("the Jews") for refusing to accept him.

How then does John depict the exact developments and circumstances that eventuate in Jesus' Roman trial? The first attempts of Jesus' adversaries to arrest him or kill him are spontaneous or at most "semi-official." However, as 11:47-53 indicates their efforts subsequently assumed an official and a more coordinated character.[7] Given the important turn of events that is signaled by the high priest's intervention at this juncture, this passage is appropriately cited in full:

So the chief priests and the Pharisees gathered and said, "What are we to do? For this man performs many signs. If we let him go on thus, every one will believe in him, and the Romans will come and destroy both our holy place and our nation." But one of them, Caiaphas, who was high priest that year, said to them, "You know nothing at all; you do not understand that it is expedient for you that one man should die for the people, and that the whole nation should not perish." He did not say this of his own accord, but being high priest that year he prophesied that Jesus should die for the nation, and not for the nation only, but to gather into one the children of God who are scattered abroad. So from that day on they took counsel how to put him to death (11:47-53).

Perhaps the most difficult aspect to reflect about in the foregoing passage regards the degree of sincerity that John wishes to ascribe to the chief priests and the Pharisees when he reports the concluding part of their statement, " . . . and the Romans will come and destroy both our holy place and our nation." There is comparatively little difficulty in interpreting the first part of their reaction, because Jesus has just performed the major sign of healing the blind man (9:1-41) and now the unsurpassed sign of bringing Lazarus back to life (11:1-44). John's readers are thus not surprised that the chief priests and Pharisees, upon receiving the report of Lazarus' restoration (11:45-56), become alarmed that everyone may soon believe in Jesus.

But what plausibility does John want attached to his report that these adversaries feared a forceful intervention on the part of the Romans? Interestingly, this verse marks the first reference to Roman rule within John's Gospel. By including it here, John recalls to his readers that Roman rule was fundamental to the political landscape of Palestine during the time of Jesus' ministry. (Again, all of John's readers themselves live under Roman rule.) This preliminary notice regarding the Romans also functions as a kind of "bridge" to John's subsequent reports that Roman soldiers participated in the arrest of Jesus (18:30) and to his report of the actual trial before the Roman governor. Yet to what degree do Jesus' adversaries fear that the Romans will move against "our holy place" and "our nation" because of Jesus' successors? That is still the question.

When this passage is read in the context afforded by John's portrayal of these adversaries up until this point in the narrative, it is hard to conceive that John now credits them with any significant degree of sincerity. Their harsh criticism of Jesus and their machinations against him and his searing indictments of them in turn have dominated the preceding chapters. Thus it is hardly conceivable that John intends that his readers accept at face value Jesus' enemies' words that they are now acting because they altruistically fear for the preservation of the temple and the safety of the people. Rather, is it not John's sense that these adversaries are now acting because Jesus' successes greatly imperil *their own vested interests*? And is it not John's sense that they are somehow trying to persuade themselves and others as well that their motives are not craven but somehow laudatory?

The foregoing line of interpretation regarding John's subtle meaning in presenting the council members' words is extended by a similar reading of the statement by Caiaphas that John next portrays. In this interpretation Caiaphas' phrasing, ". . . it is expedient for you that one man should die, . . ." is of central importance because, in effect, the self-interest of the conspirators comes closer to the surface. Caiaphas' words indicate that it is expedient *for them* that Jesus should die.[8] What then is the force of his further intimation that Jesus die " . . . for the people, that the whole nation would not perish"?

Clearly the evangelist is interested in these words as representing an unintended prophecy regarding the salvific consequence of Jesus' death for the Jewish people and for the children of God everywhere. That meaning is unmistakable given the explicit editorial comment that John himself makes in the immediately following verse. Still, how does John precisely understand the meaning of Caiaphas' words as words uttered to the Sanhedrin? The answer is that, at this level of meaning, Caiaphas' words represent nothing less than a cynical formulation of a cover story to be used in justifying the Sanhedrin's formal initiatives to destroy Jesus.[9]

In effect then, the fundamental dynamic of Caiaphas' intervention is to chide his fellow Sanhedrin members for ineffective handwringing about what is to be done. It is to their fundamental interest that Jesus be eliminated. And any popular outcry arising from the Sanhedrin's initiative against him will be met by the response that they were forced to act in order to avert a catastrophic Roman intervention that would jeopardize the entire nation.

John's next report and one several verses later witness to the fact that Caiaphas' emphatic intervention was favorably received and galvanized the Sanhedrin into formal measures against Jesus. "So from that day on they took counsel how to put him to death," John tells his readers in 11:53. And then, using terminology that suggests that a formal warrant was issued against Jesus, John states, "Now the chief priests and the Pharisees had given orders that if any one knew where he was, he should let them know, so that they might arrest him" (11:57).

Given the necessary limitations of this study and the fact that John's Roman trial account remains the primary concern of the present chapter, only brief mention can be made at this time to two developments that occur within John's narrative between this point and Jesus' appearance before Pilate more than five chapters later. Both of these items shed important light upon the circumstances under which Jesus arrived at Pilate's praetorium.

The first of these narrative developments centers upon the initial lack of success that the chief priests and Pharisees have in their efforts to apprehend Jesus. Throughout the Gospel John portrays Jesus acting in such a way that his adversaries are kept off balance regarding his movements and his intentions, and this *modus operandi* is evident here as well. John relates that Jesus no longer went about openly but rather withdrew with his disciples "to the country near the wilderness, to a town called Ephraim"

(11:54). After an interval, though, he traveled once more to Bethany, proximate to Jerusalem, to the house of Martha, Mary and Lazarus (12:1). At this point John's sense is that Jesus once again comes under surveillance from his adversaries (12:10). However, despite this surveillance, his enemies are powerless to prevent him from receiving a great welcome and royal acclaim when he enters Jerusalem on the next day (12:12-19).

The second narrative development centers upon the role of Judas and Satan in achieving the arrest of Jesus. The chief priests and Pharisees were virtually powerless at the time of Jesus' entry. However, within *days*, they have him in custody and on trial before the Roman governor. When John's account is read closely with a view to explaining the adversaries' sudden success against Jesus, it emerges that John never explicitly mentions any formal or even informal contact between the chief priests and the Roman administration prior to Jesus' arrest. In contrast, what John does indicate is that Judas' betrayal of Jesus (a betrayal influenced by Satan; see 13:2,27,30) was the critical factor in allowing the chief priests and Pharisees to apprehend Jesus and bring him to trial.

When Judas departs from the final supper, John does not relate that Judas left in order to conspire with the chief priests and the Pharisees. Nor, as just mentioned, does John indicate that there were prior contacts by these parties with the Roman authorities regarding Jesus. Nevertheless, from John's description of the arrest that subsequently took place in a secluded garden across the Kidron valley, it emerges that these contacts have been made. For, when Judas arrives upon that scene, he has with him attendants (guards) from the chief priests and Pharisees *and* a cohort of Roman soldiers with their tribune (18:3,12).[10] After at first being disoriented by Jesus' sovereign presence, this arresting party recovers its purpose, seizes Jesus, and leads him bound to the high priest Annas (18:12-13).

2. INTERACTIONS BETWEEN JESUS' ADVERSARIES AND PILATE

After his arrest Jesus was taken to Annas, who asked questions about Jesus' disciples and his teaching only to have him respond with an indignant, even defiant declaration (18:13,19-23). Annas then sent Jesus bound to Caiaphas (18:24), and from there Jesus was subsequently taken to Pontius Pilate's praetorium (18:28).

As is well known, John's portrayal of Jesus' trial before Pilate has a dramatic quality to it. Like an actor moving between two locations on a single stage, Pilate is shown to move back and forth between Jesus' adversaries, who remain outside the praetorium, and Jesus, who is under guard inside.[11] It should be noted that John's descriptions of these interactions are exceedingly complex and that a clear appreciation for the outcome that emerges can only be gained by giving careful attention to the gradual shifts that Pilate makes as the drama unfolds.

From the standpoint of the present study, the multifaceted assertions of his own sovereignty that Jesus makes to Pilate are of primary interest and will be treated separately in the next section of this chapter. Nevertheless, because they supply important data to John's readers as to the outcome of Jesus' public ministry and because they also obviously supply the immediate context for Jesus' interactions with Pilate, it is important to analyze the principal points that John presents in detailing Jesus' adversaries' encounter with Pilate. Finally, the fact that loyalty to Caesar emerges so prominently at the end of these encounters also makes them of more than passing interest.

Because this material is complex, it will be useful to provide a general overview of the parties' interactions before delving into a more detailed exegesis of the specific exchanges. In particular, three characteristics of John's narrative are to be observed: (a) that throughout the proceedings Jesus' adversaries remain absolutely uncompromising in their demand for his execution; (b) that they sequentially shift their charges against him until they finally arrive at a charge and at a threat that proves effective with Pilate; and (c) that while Pilate gradually loses his dominant position, he still retains sufficient leverage to ensure that the chief priests debase themselves as the price for Jesus' death.

Keeping these considerations in mind, it is now possible to delve more deeply into the particular exchanges between Pilate and Jesus' adversaries that John reports. Essentially John reports six of these interchanges with each except the last ending in such a way that Pilate remains face to face with the demand for Jesus' execution.

In the first interchange (18:28b-31), Jesus' adversaries confront Pilate[12] with the accusation that Jesus is an "evildoer," that is, a criminal.[13] Pilate's initial response to them indicates his refusal to become involved in a matter pertaining to Jewish law. However, Jesus' opponents counter that he must enter the proceedings because they are seeking nothing less than a sentence of death against Jesus.[14]

The second interchange with the adversaries (18:38b-40) occurs after Pilate has had a somewhat extended exchange with Jesus. (As indicated, Pilate's dialogues with Jesus will be treated below; however, it is noted here that Pilate's interrogation of Jesus has turned on the issue of whether he is "the king of the Jews.")[15] The governor declares that he finds Jesus guilty of no crime and offers the adversaries a face-saving way for them to retreat from their demand. While he is rejecting their case, he nevertheless proposes that he release Jesus, "the king of the Jews" (18:39b), not by an outright dismissal of the charges but rather by the utilization of an existing custom.[16] Adamantly, the adversaries reject this offer and then squelch any use of this "Passover" custom to free Jesus by demanding that Barabbas be the one released under this provision.

The third interchange occurs after Pilate has ordered Jesus' scourging and his soldiers have mocked him with the derisive, "Hail, king of the Jews" (19:1-2). Opening this scene, Pilate reiterates to the adversaries that he finds no crime in Jesus and presents him to them scourged and mocked and now wearing a crown of thorns (19:4-5a). Pilate's famous words in presenting Jesus to them, "Behold the man," appear designed to win a measure of sympathy for Jesus as one who has been dealt with severely, with a view to gaining his release (19:5a).[17] However, the chief priests and their attendants remain unmollified by Jesus' condition and raise the chant, "Crucify him, crucify him" (19:6a).

The fourth interchange then follows immediately (19:6b-8). The briefest of the six alternations, it is also the one that is least susceptible to succinct summary. In context, Pilate's statement to the chief priests that they should take and crucify Jesus themselves essentially emphasizes his own position as *the only one* possessing authority and power for crucifixion. And even as his statement reminds Jesus' adversaries of this, it also re-emphasizes to them that Pilate does not find Jesus guilty of any crime requiring death. In light of the preceding chants to crucify Jesus, Pilate's present declaration indicates his own continued refusal to do so.

However, again Jesus' adversaries are intransigent. They emphatically insist that Jesus must die, now giving as the rationale for his execution that he had made himself the Son of God. John then indicates that, upon hearing these words, Pilate was "the more afraid" (19:8b). The exact meaning of this latter phrase has proved elusive, but it may be John's sense that Pilate now became increasingly uneasy about his own role in the proceedings once he heard this reference to Jesus' exalted status.[18]

It is the fifth exchange between Pilate and Jesus' opponents that first signals the turn toward Jesus' execution. In the aftermath of his final dialogue with Jesus, Pilate sought once again to release him. However, at this juncture Jesus' adversaries pressed a new charge against him, coupling it with a threat to denounce Pilate to Caesar. And Pilate then began to retreat from his previously strong declamations that Jesus should be released!

As John reports them, the charge and the threat reinforce each other, and loyalty to Caesar is a central moment in each. The charge, expressed in the second part of their response to Pilate, transposed a title that was initially used by Pilate, and then subsequently used as an epithet by his soldiers. That title, of course, was "the king of the Jews." And now the chief priests' charge against Jesus is that he is a king against Caesar:[19] "Every one who makes himself a king sets himself against Caesar" (19:12b).

Jesus' adversaries accompanied this charge with an ominous, scarcely concealed threat. Although John never expressly states that Pilate was shaken by the threat of being denounced to Caesar, such a consequence is implicitly recorded as his narrative now moves forward and Pilate ends by handing Jesus to his soldiers for crucifixion. It is therefore appropriate that this threat[20] be explicitly cited: "If you release this man, you are not Caesar's friend" (19:12a).

The final interchange that John describes should be regarded as a careful portrayal of how a Roman governor, at once powerful and threatened, finally acceded to the pressure of Jesus' intransigent adversaries for his death.[21] Pontius Pilate, the Roman governor in question, did accede to the chief priests' demand. However he did not do so without first exacting a price of his own from them.

In contrast with the circumstances of several of the preceding interchanges, John does not here depict Pilate interacting further with Jesus before proceeding. Rather, in 19:13 John portrays Pilate acting directly in response to the adversaries' threat. He brings Jesus out for formal judgment and seems to be on the verge of sentencing him to crucifixion. Yet he undertakes two additional steps.

Pilate's first move can be regarded as a final attempt to gain Jesus' release. Earlier he attempted to gain sympathy for Jesus by presenting him with the words, "Behold the man." Now he presents Jesus with the words, "Behold your king." In the former instance Jesus' adversaries cried, "Crucify him, crucify him." Now, still unrelenting, their cry is, "Away with him, away with him, crucify him" (19:15).

The intent of Pilate's second step only becomes clear when the full meaning of the response that it elicits from Jesus' adversaries is reflected upon. Pilate's next words "Shall I crucify your King?" (19:15b)[22] mark a critical turn in the proceedings. His receptiveness to Jesus' execution is now indicated, yet he continues to play upon the term "king", seemingly in an effort to have his own position respected. So intent are Jesus' adversaries upon his death—is this not the sense of John's scene at this point—that they now abjectly demean themselves in order to overcome this last obstacle,[23] the Roman governor's insistence that his own prerogatives be verbally respected.

What is the response that the chief priests give to Pilate's provocative reference to Jesus as their king? It is the craven, self-debasing protestation: "We have no king but Caesar" (19:15c). John then reports that upon hearing these words Pilate handed Jesus over for crucifixion.

In effect, then, the chief priests have won their objective, Jesus' death. Nevertheless, while having had to turn from his own conviction about Jesus under their pressure, Pilate still has managed to maintain vestiges of his prerogatives as governor. As the narrative proceeds, he additionally asserts these prerogatives by refusing imperiously to accede to the chief priests' request that the wording of the inscription on Jesus' cross be altered (19:19-22).

3. JESUS' SOVEREIGNTY MANIFESTED BEFORE PILATE

As noted in the preceding chapter, John's Gospel is permeated by references to Jesus' sovereign standing from the prologue forward. These references are intensified, if anything, in the descriptions that John now provides regarding Jesus' arrest, his trial before Pilate, and his death. Indeed, the passages pertaining to these events are so alloyed with indications of Jesus' sovereignty that a full presentation of this aspect cannot be undertaken within the space available here. The paragraphs that follow should thus be regarded as an attempt to treat only certain elements in John's presentation of Jesus' sovereignty. Also, the formal task of correlating John's trial narrative with the presumed experiences and sensibilities of his readers will not be undertaken until the following chapter.

With respect to John's arrest scene, it should be noted how fully sovereign Jesus is before the arresting party. John relates that Jesus knew in advance what would befall him and took the initiative in addressing the arresting party (18:4). When he identified himself to them, stating "I am he," those in the arresting party drew back and fell to the ground (18:6). Following this, Jesus asked again whom they were seeking and then mandated the release of his disciples in fulfillment of his earlier word (18:7-9). Finally, in rebuking Peter for striking with the sword, Jesus emphasized that he himself was consciously choosing to drink from the cup which the Father had given him (18:11).

At a general level two things may be said with respect to the dialogues between Jesus and Pilate that John relates within the framework of his longer trial narrative. Negatively, Jesus is neither obsequious before nor intimidated by Pilate. Positively, he takes the "interrogation" into channels of his own choosing, using Pilate's questions as a vehicle for the communication of his own truth. In both dialogues Jesus' sovereign standing is amply delineated. In both dialogues Jesus' bearing and response make an impact upon Pilate even though this Roman prefect succumbs in the end to the pressure of Jesus' adversaries.

In John's description the first dialogue (18:33-38) is the longer of the two and consists essentially in a central question with two related questions by Pilate and three responses by Jesus. Within John's framework Pilate's great question, "Are you the king of the Jews?" establishes a fundamental category for the rest of the interrogation and for the remainder of the passion narrative.[24] Jesus' initial response, asking Pilate a counter-question, also sets the tone for much that follows. It is so assertive, so independent as to border on being confrontational: "Do you say this of your own accord, or did others say it to you about me?" (18:34).[25]

Pilate imperiously brushes this response aside and re-commences his interrogation (18:35). At this point Jesus' reply is relatively extended. Given in a somewhat complex "A-B-A" form, it provides important perspectives on his own self-understanding of his kingly role. His response especially emphasizes and explains that his own kingly rule must be distinguished from the type of militarily based rule that Pilate envisions in his question about the "king of the Jews." For Jesus' reign is "not of this world" and "not from the world" (18:36a, 36c).[26]

Importantly, the evidence for these assertions is supplied by the fact that Jesus' servants[27] have not fought to oppose his arrest: " . . . if my kingship were of this world, my servants would fight that I might not be handed over to the Jews" (18:36b). Jesus, then, does not seek to supplant Roman rule in Judea through force of arms.

At this juncture Pilate questioningly surmises that Jesus must then be a king (18:37). In his reply Jesus again implicitly acknowledges that he is a king, but once again insists upon his own meaning of that term. In this instance he refers to his pre-existence and incarnation and stresses that his kingship is focused upon bearing witness to the truth: "You say that I am a king. For this I was born, and for this I have come into the world, to bear witness to the truth" (18:37a). Essentially then, Jesus' kingdom is a kingdom that has to do with truth and his kingly role involves bearing witness to the truth.

The final sentence in Jesus' response, "Every one who is of the truth hears my voice" (18:37b), carries a subtle note of invitation for Pilate to acept Jesus' words and his authority.[28] And thus does John portray Jesus epitomizing his sovereignty. Jesus, the prisoner whose kingship is not to be reckoned in Roman terms, now moves to invite Pilate, his judge, to acknowledge a kingship defined in Jesus' terms. The final aspects of John's scene suggest that Jesus' words have engaged Pilate in some way. There is a reflective element to Pilate's concluding question "What is truth?" (18:38). And the governor then goes out to Jesus' adversaries intent on releasing him.

Jesus' second dialogue with Pilate (19:9-11) resumes the discussion of Jesus' origin and then broadens in focus to indicate the limits of Pilate's power in a larger framework that is essentially ordered *from above*.

Pilate's initial question to Jesus, "Where do you come from?" (19:9a), is at least in part prompted by his own personal unease about Jesus. John states expressly that Jesus refused to answer this question and implies the stance of someone with superior standing not deigning to answer the query of someone lower. Pilate clearly regards such a response as outrageous given his own estimation of the Roman power he wields: "You will not speak to me? Do you not know that I have power to release you, and power to crucify you?" (19:10).

At this stage John's portrayal of Jesus' sovereignty is particularly memorable. Jesus does not consider that he is dependent upon Pilate for his life, and he is not intimidated by Pilate's brandishing of his powers. The nuances of the original Greek are somewhat difficult to capture in English translation. However, the actual force of Jesus' reply is to witness to Pilate concerning the existence of a higher order. Thus, far from negotiating with Pilate for his life, Jesus confronts the governor with the fact that he would have no power over him unless Jesus' betrayal had been permitted to occur in accordance with the Father's ordered plan.[29]

Further, the meaning of Jesus' statement is not that Pilate is thereby exonerated from sin for his role in the proceedings. Rather, it is that, within the framework given from above, the preeminent guilt belongs to those who have betrayed Jesus and handed him over.[30] In the citation of this passage now given, an insertion is made in an effort to communicate more carefully the meaning of the Greek text on both of these points; i.e., the Father's ordered framework and the relative degree of guilt involved:

> You would have no power over me unless it [this framework of events] had been given you from above; therefore he who delivered me to you has the greater sin (19:11).

As previously mentioned, at the conclusion of this second dialogue John again shows Pilate to have been significantly influenced by what had transpired. However, as considered previously, Pilate, faced with the intransigence of Jesus' adversaries, ultimately betrayed his own convictions and handed Jesus over for crucifixion.

4. JESUS' SOVEREIGNTY IN CRUCIFIXION AND IN DEATH

The concept of Jesus' kingship continues as a significant element within the larger portrayal of Jesus' sovereignty that John provides in describing the circumstances of Jesus' death and burial. Kingship will accordingly be the subject of the initial paragraphs of this section and will be followed in turn by a brief treatment of several other indications of Jesus' continuing sovereignty.

John indicates in 19:17-18 that, pursuant to the governor's orders, Roman soldiers took Jesus to Golgotha and crucified him there along with two others. Significantly, Pilate wrote a titulus for Jesus' cross giving the grounds for his execution. This titulus, "Jesus of Nazareth the King of the Jews," stated formally that Jesus was being crucified for the offense of subversion.[31] However, John's descriptions of Pilate in the preceding and subsequent passages also establishes a second facet of meaning beyond this formal aspect. Pilate is in effect personally affirming that something about Jesus *is* kingly.[32]

This second dimension of meaning is attested to by the vigorous negative reaction that John attributes to the chief priests in 19:21. Their demand to Pilate is that he change the wording so that no suggestion be given that Jesus is a king; rather, let the titulus read minimally that Jesus *claimed* to be a king of the Jews. Regarding the circumstances of their request, John suggests that the priests were galvanized by the fact that many Jews were reading this inscription since it was written in Hebrew, Latin, and Greek (19:20). However, as previously noted, Pilate haughtily refused to accede to their petition.

What then is to be said with respect to John's overall portrayal of Jesus' kingly identity? It can be suggested here that this topic presumably held more than minimal interest to John's readers throughout the Roman empire. Do John's various reports supply a coherent presentation of this aspect of Jesus' identity? This is the question to be briefly considered.

In the previous analysis of Jesus' dialogue with Pilate, it has been observed that Jesus affirmed his own kingship but stressed that his reign was "not of this world" and would not be established through violent means. Instead, his kingship was oriented toward truth and involved him in witness to the truth. Coming as they do in a formal trial before one who holds Roman *imperium*, these pronouncements by Jesus mark the culmination of the references to the subject of kingly rule that have preceded in the narrative of the Gospel. However, when the three earlier references to this topic are analyzed, what emerges is that Jesus has twice previously *acted* in a manner consistent with the premises that he now articulates in his testimony before Pilate.

Before proceeding to the two principal passages that serve to delineate Jesus' stance in this matter, an initial occurrence in which Jesus accepts "king of Israel" as a term of acclaim should be mentioned. In the first chapter of the Gospel, at the outset of his ministry, Jesus is acclaimed with exalted titles by John the Baptist and several of his first disciples, Nathaniel included. Impressed by Jesus' clairvoyant remark to him, Nathaniel responds: "Rabbi, you are the Son of God! You are the King of Israel!" (1:49). As just mentioned, Jesus' response is to accept this title, even as he briefly instructs Nathaniel regarding other dimensions of belief (1:50-51).

Yet if this passage indicates Jesus' acceptance of kingly standing, subsequent passages in chapters 6 and 12 demonstrate that his acceptance of this title and role will not involve him in replacing Roman rule with his own political reign. This issue, in effect, is the issue that arose in the wake of Jesus' powerful sign in feeding the five thousand with five barley loaves and two fish (6:1-13). The response of the people assembled is to view Jesus as God's definitive prophet (6:14) and to try to force him to be king. Jesus, however, rejects this attempt to install him as a political ruler. For as John reports: "Perceiving then that they were about to come and take him by force to make him king, Jesus withdrew again to the mountain by himself" (6:15).

A somewhat comparable situation involving a large crowd publicly giving acclamation to Jesus as a king is also described by John in chapter 12. Here the preceding context has included Jesus' definitive sign in restoring Lazarus to life. And now the crowd of Passover pilgrims welcomes Jesus into Jerusalem with the palm branches used for hailing victors and the cry, "Hosanna! Blessed is he who comes in the name of the Lord, even the King of Israel!" (12:13).

What response does Jesus give to this popular acclaim for him as a king? In John's report his response is a symbolic action chosen specifically to dispel any sentiments that his purpose in arriving in Jerusalem was to inaugurate political rule. Jesus' symbolic deed was to secure a young ass (the antithesis of a war stallion or a military chariot) and make his entry into the city in a gentle fashion. In effect, such a startling step could only serve to dampen any nationalist expectation on the part of the crowd while still allowing them the opportunity for suitable acclaim. John's own citation of a Scripture text derived substantially from Zechariah 9:9 interprets the meaning of this action in unmistakable terms for his readers: "Fear not, daughter of Zion; behold your king is coming, sitting on an ass's colt!" (12:14b). Jesus is indeed arriving as a king, but *not* as one whose kingship is "of this world."

In the verses following this citation John states that initially Jesus' disciples did not understand this event, *"but when Jesus was glorified*, then they remembered that this had been written of him and had been done to him" (12:16; italics added). This concept of Jesus being glorified is perhaps an appropriate construct with which to move to some of the other aspects of Jesus' sovereign standing that complement his identity as a king. For "glorification" is one way of expressing the fundamental meaning that John the evangelist espouses as he describes the events pertaining to Jesus' crucifixion and death. It is John's thesis, in effect, that Jesus is not being destroyed by these events but is instead being "lifted up" by them and is glorified in them.[33]

John provides additional indications of Jesus' sovereignty in his descriptions of the circumstances of Jesus' death and burial, and at least a cursory treatment should be given here before concluding.[34] Beginning with Jesus' time on the cross, perhaps the first point to be observed is John's portrayal of Jesus' sovereignly providing care for his mother and the beloved disciple (19:26-27). Jesus' solicitude in this scene recalls the solicitude he earlier exhibited in providing for his disciples' safety at the time of his arrest (18:8b).

John then indicates that, after he had made this important provision, Jesus knew that *all* was now accomplished (19:28a). This report again emphasizes that Jesus retained a sovereign consciousness regarding all aspects of his mission right to the very end.

Then, because he wished to have the Scriptures fulfilled, Jesus expressed his thirst (19:28). Once again, Jesus is in the position of one consciously initiating steps that are in accordance with God's will. After receiving this proffered drink, he gave formal, even public, expression to this consciousness as to the accomplishment of his mission by stating solemnly: "It is finished" (19:30a). Upon these words he then bowed his head and autonomously gave up his spirit (19:30b).[35]

Dying in such a manner, Jesus was spared the experience of having his legs broken to hasten death; John again adduces a scriptural text to indicate the felicitousness of this outcome (19:31-33,36). Similarly, the remarkable event of blood and water flowing from his side when it was pierced also is interpreted favorably by John (19:34-35,37). In short within John's framework, Jesus' dignity, Jesus' sovereign bearing, Jesus' autonomy remain untarnished even though he undergoes all of the specific aspects of Roman crucifixion.

This same fundamental consideration also prevails with respect to Jesus' burial as it is described by John. Two men of standing, Joseph of Arimathea and Nicodemus, intervene to accord him a careful, reverent burial. They use a generous amount of the burial spices, bind Jesus' body with strips of linen, and bury him alone in a new garden tomb. In summary, Jesus who exhibited such startling majesty throughout his life and even in his death, is now the recipient of a dignified and reverent burial. Indeed such a burial testifies[36] to one whose standing is that of a king.

6

Jesus' Farewell Discourses

An initial word is in order regarding the structure of the present chapter and its relationship to the chapters that precede and follow it in this study. To take the latter topic first, it is apparent that a decision has been taken to treat chapters 13 to 17 of John's Gospel out of their chronological sequence. What is the rationale for such a step? Fundamentally, it is a step taken from a desire to consider Jesus' farewell sharings with his disciple *after* the outcome of the public ministry has been analyzed in detail. Indeed, Jesus' final discourses are so rich in meaning for the present study that their analysis might even have been deferred for consideration until Jesus' resurrection appearances themselves had been treated.

Second, the internal structure of this chapter itself deserves attention. There are only three sections within the present chapter, and two of them are concerned with assessing the implications of John's account for Christians living within the context of Roman rule. The content of these two sections is different, however. Section one below uses extremely broad strokes in relating leading features of Jesus' sovereignty from the body of the Gospel and from the trial narrative to the situation of John's readership. In contrast, section three examines the implications of key themes from Jesus' farewell addresses after these have been carefully analyzed in section two.

1. JOHN'S PORTRAYAL OF JESUS: INITIAL REFLECTIONS

Chapters four and five of this study have identified numerous features of John's account that emphasize the sovereign status of Jesus. It is now time to summarize these features and to suggest some of their implications for the readers of the Gospel who lived within the context of Roman rule.

That the Roman system of rule relied heavily upon the sovereignty of the Roman emperor is a fundamental datum that must be kept constantly in mind. In this connection, the claims and practices of the various emperors with respect to their semi-divine or divine status should also be recalled.

Chapters two and three established that there were both potential and real points of clash between representatives of these imperial claims and members of the new Christian movement. These chapters accorded particular attention to developments regarding the tax against Jews that Vespasian imposed and also considered in some detail the astounding practices whereby Nero was hailed as "savior of the world" and Domitian claimed to be "lord and god." Key aspects in the persecution and trials of Christians in Bithynia-Pontus, and especially the fact that Pliny mentioned earlier official trials in his letter to Trajan, also received proportionate attention.

Parenthetically, it can be noted at this juncture that a more extended investigation of the self-aggrandizing claims of the earlier emperors (Nero in particular) could be undertaken if it were the present study's objective to document just how extensively imperial claims inimical to Christians were being advanced prior to the Flavian emperors. Thus it should not be supposed that the arguments now to be advanced regarding John's affirmation of Jesus' sovereignty only have relevance within a Flavian or post-Flavian context.

Reading and reflecting upon this Gospel within circumstances in which the emperor's sovereignty was significantly emphasized, what a contrasting view of reality, what alternative truths, John's readers would have found within his account! In essence, they would have found a view of reality in which Christ's position and power are unquestionably paramount. And they would have found reports about Christ's kingship and witness to the truth that were starkly in contrast with the prevailing Roman worldview.

From all that has been previously discussed, it is evident that John's readers would have found a steady emphasis upon Jesus' exalted identity as the Son of God. With God from the beginning, he witnessed with authority and sovereignty at every stage of his earthly journey. So intensive is this emphasis upon Jesus' sovereign rule within the Gospel that it actually mattered little with what section of John's account his readers might commence. Whether they listened to a public reading of John's prologue, reflected upon Jesus' early signs and discourses, considered his raising of Lazarus, pondered his kingly bearing throughout his passion, or meditated upon resurrection passages attesting to his transformed life and return to the Father, John's audience could not have bypassed the evangelist's overriding message concerning Jesus' sovereign status and role.

Within a context of Roman imperial claims and within a context in which some members of John's audience may have been under the threat of denunciation and trial, the evangelist's emphatic upholding of Christ's sovereignty beyond any sovereign entity of "the world" could only inspire a renewed dedication and commitment to Jesus. It was, of course, Jesus and not Nero or any other emperor who was truly *Savior of the world*. It was, of course, Jesus and not Domitian or any other emperor who was truly *Lord and God*. No Roman emperor of any age, but only Jesus shows the way to the Father and the life that is everlasting.

What also should be recognized at this juncture is that John's Roman trial narrative certainly would have received the riveted attention of any of his readers for whom Roman legal proceedings were a reality or even a possibility. As believers in Jesus, as disciples deeply committed to upholding his sovereignty, John's readers would have found within the trial narrative a fundamental reply for them to give to the Roman authorities who interrogated them. Their reply: that as disciples of Jesus they had no objective of violently contesting against Roman rule.

While they might sincerely give such a response to their Roman judges, presumably in at least some cases it would prove insufficient for achieving their acquittal. This too was a situation provided for in John's account. Despite *his* innocence, the evil of Jesus' adversaries and the negativity of "the world" influenced Pilate to betray the truth and give a capital sentence against Jesus. John's readers would be well established on this point and also well oriented to the fact that Jesus had resisted Pilate's effort to intimidate him and had even reminded Pilate regarding the limits of his power. In imitation of Jesus' own conduct, so might his later disciples resist Roman intimidation and seek to bear witness to the truth.

That this witness to the truth meant an unwavering testimony that Jesus is the true Lord and true Savior of the world obviously had the potential for controversial and highly charged tribunal proceedings. The putative situation of later Christians facing such Roman proceedings with John's Gospel in hand as a major resource is thus one that admits of considerable complexity. Even now the analysis of how John's account responded to this situation is far from complete; important passages in the farewell discourse chapters and key passages in John's concluding chapters still need to be assessed.

2. KEY CONCEPTS FROM JESUS' FAREWELL DISCOURSES

It is well known that John 13-17 describes Jesus' washing of his disciples' feet and then recounts a series of dialogues and extended discourses. The profound sentiments expressed by Jesus at this time indeed have the potential for being meaningfully contemplated within a variety of settings. Yet, for the purposes of the present study it is appropriate to approach these discourses on the premise that, in part, John envisioned them as being read by Christians who were under the threat of Roman persecution.

Proceeding on this basis, there are at least five topics touched upon in Jesus' farewell discourses that should now be considered. These topics are: (a) Jesus' words concerning persecution; (b) his warning regarding apostasy; (c) his insistence that his disciples remain closely bonded with him; (d) his insistence that they love one another; and (e) his words conveying particular assurances. Inasmuch as these discourses frequently repeat key themes and key ideas, the presentation that will now be made freely draws upon material from the beginning, middle, and concluding sections of Jesus' addresses.

Jesus' statements on the theme of persecution are given at 15:18-16:4a and 16:32-33 of the discourses and, carefully assessed, refer primarily to persecution at the hands of the religious authorities.[1] In Johannine scholarship a great amount of attention has been devoted to assessing the attitudes and practices of official Judaism that may have been influential with John as he finalized this section of his narrative.[2] However, as the following section will explicate, what is of fundamental importance from the perspective of this study is simply the fact that Jesus predicts to his disciples that they themselves will be persecuted. As indicated, he does this at two points within the discourse:

If they persecuted me, they *will persecute you* (15:20; italics added).

In the world *you* have *persecution* (16:33; italics added).

What is also of fundamental importance is that Jesus explains his motive for wanting his disciples to be informed regarding this future experience. It is that, forewarned, they will not apostasize in the face of this persecution.[3] And thus his words to them at the beginning of chapter 16, attesting to his concern that they not yield when threatened:

I have said this to you to keep you from falling away (16:1).

But I have said these things to you, that when their hour comes you may remember that I told you of them (16:4).

Given the Fourth Gospel's steady emphasis upon belief, it is hardly possible to overemphasize the significance of Jesus' words alerting his disciples regarding a temptation to apostasize. Yet these words assume a still greater significance when they are considered within the context of numerous other concepts within the farewell discourses. One of these related concepts concerns the importance of staying closely bonded with Jesus.

Jesus' counsel to his disciples that they should "remain" in him is present in other settings within the Gospel.[4] However, within his farewell discourses, Jesus richly develops this point by imaging himself as the true vine and the disciples as the branches. This image is set forth at the beginning of chapter 15 (15:1-11). It, in turn, supplies the framework[5] for his urging that the disciples are to love one another (15:12,17), his avowal that there is not a greater love than to lay down one's life for one's friends[6] (15:13), and his dramatic insistence that his disciples are now his friends (15:14-15).

As indicated previously, reflections on the implications of key concepts contained within the farewell discourse will be presented in the third section of this chapter. However, in this instance it seems desirable not to defer reflection upon two aspects of the material contained in John 15. Both of these aspects would have been highly significant to recipients of the Gospel who were facing Roman persecution. The first aspect relates to the fundamental concept of striving to remain closely bonded with Jesus. As powerful as Jesus' words that he is the true vine are for Christians facing the ordinary challenges of discipleship, they are even more encouraging when read and shared by Christians under the threat of persecution.

It is useful simply to present three or four verses from this section of Jesus' discourses. This section in its entirety, fifteen verses, can be envisioned as constituting a powerful resource for meditation and prayer by individual Christians or by a gathered Christian community threatened by the authorities. Statements of Jesus such as these do indeed take on a powerful and poignant meaning when they are read and reflected upon by disciples facing persecution:[7]

> Abide in me and I in you. As the branch cannot bear fruit by itself unless it abides in the vine, neither can you unless you abide in me (15:4).

> I am the vine and you are the branches. Those who abide in me and I in them bear much fruit, because apart from me you can do nothing (15:5).

> By this my Father is glorified, that you bear much fruit, and so prove to be my disciples. As the Father has loved me, so have I loved you; abide in my love (15:8-9).

The second aspect of chapter 15 that would seemingly have possessed particular relevance for John's readers is that of Jesus' invitation to friendship. Conceptually this image of friendship with Jesus functions to intensify and enhance the former image of abiding with him. Situated within the context of the vine-branches image and two assertions that they must love another, Jesus' fundamental statement conferring the status of *friends* upon his disciples is the following:

> No longer do I call you servants, for the servant does not know what his master is doing; but I have called you friends, for all that I have heard from my Father I have made known to you (15:15).

Viewed within the framework of John's larger account, this image of friendship with Jesus can also be understood as functioning to provide a stark contrast with yet another important image. Here attention must be directed back to the last chapter's analysis of John's trial narrative. As indicated then, the chief priests and the Pharisees repeatedly sought a charge or some hold upon Pilate in order to force Jesus' crucifixion. After several failed attempts they finally found the lever needed. This they expressed in their hurled epithet: "You are not Caesar's friend" (19:12b).

To be sure, no explicit contrast between these two concepts—"friend of Jesus" and "friend of Caesar"—is made within the Gospel itself. Rather, they are simply presented as concepts that are respectively important for the meaning of Jesus' farewell to his disciples and for the meaning of his Roman trial. Nevertheless, if John's readers meditated upon these two images in the face of Roman persecution, they would have derived considerable guidance and sustenance. They, unalterably called to friendship with Jesus, were to distance themselves from the likes of Pilate—Pilate who so highly prized being regarded as a friend of Caesar that he was willing to execute Jesus! Almost parenthetically, it can also be suggested that this line of meditation might have led them to a similar fruitful juxtaposition of the two contrasting declarations, "We have no king but Caesar" (19:15b) and "Jesus of Nazareth, the King of the Jews" (19:19b).

Before proceeding to the other important elements present within these discourses, one additional statement by Jesus pertaining to friendship should be considered: "No one has greater love than this, to lay down one's life for one's friends" (15:13). Again, how powerful a meaning does such a statement assume if the context for the Christian reader or Christian community reading and hearing it is that of approaching martyrdom!

Within the larger framework of the farewell discourses the concept of abiding in friendship with Jesus easily blends into the concept of the love that the disciples are to have for one another. In 14:34a Jesus speaks of a "new" commandment that he is now entrusting to his disciples. This commandment is that they shall love one another even as Jesus has loved them (15:12).[8] Indeed this love for one another shall be a mark identifying them as Jesus' disciples. Others shall know that these are authentically Jesus' disciples by reason of the love they manifest for one another (14:35).

Within this same supper setting it is obvious that Jesus' washing of his disciples' feet is intended to serve as a concrete reference point for what it means to express love for one another—"If I then, your Teacher and Lord, have washed your feet, you also ought to wash one another's feet" (13:14). As noted previously, Jesus' later words on friendship and laying down one's life for one's friends in chapter 15 are effectively bracketed by two almost identical injunctions "commanding" the disciples to love one another (15:12,17). The disciples' call to love one another is thus well attested to within Jesus' final discourses.

The analysis of the key concepts in chapters 13 through 17 now arrives at the final heading of Jesus' specific assurances and encouragement for the situation that his disciples will find themselves in after his departure. The material to be treated at this point certainly does not constitute a set of concepts that are to be rigorously distinguished from the other concepts previously treated in this section. Rather, there is a degree of overlapping and dissolving as to the boundary lines of these various concepts. Again, with a regard for methodology it should be observed that, even upon completion of this treatment of Jesus' assurances, the rich content of the farewell discourses will be far from exhausted.

In considering Jesus' assurances and his encouragement for the disciples, the initial element to be emphasized is his explanation that his departure fulfills the Father's plan and will benefit the disciples. Along with 13:3, John 16:28 contains Jesus' fundamental statement on this subject of his coming and going: "I came from the Father and have come into the world; again, I am leaving the world and going to the Father." Moreover, in both 14:1-3 and 14:18-20 Jesus movingly seeks to allay the disciples fears and encourages their trust. The former of these passages is now appropriately cited:

> Let not your hearts be troubled; believe in God, believe also in me. In my Father's house are many rooms; if it were not so, would I have told you that I go to prepare a place for you? And when I go and prepare a place for you, I will come again and will take you to myself, that where I am you may be also (14:1-3).

The second specific area in which Jesus can be seen to give assurance to his disciples concerns the continuing presence of the evil one, Satan.[9] The presence of Satan has been adverted to earlier in John's account (6:70; 12:31) and Satan was also shown to have influence over Judas during the course of the supper (13:27). Nevertheless, while adverting to Satan's arrival (14:30a), Jesus unalterably proclaims: "He has no power over me" (14:30b). This proclamation is itself fully consistent with two other proclamations by Jesus that a judgment will be made against "the ruler of this world" (12:31; 16:11).

Significantly, Jesus later also expressly prays that his disciples be preserved from the evil one. His disciples will still remain in the world after his departure and will have to contend with the presence of evil. Jesus does not minimize the seriousness of this situation. However, his prayer is that the disciples will still be kept free from the influence of Satan:

> I do not pray that thou shouldst take them out of the world, but that thou shouldst keep them from the evil one (17:15).

One of Jesus' proclamations that judgment will be made against "the ruler of this world" (16:11) is deserving of further attention because of the agent named to perform this judgment. This "agent" is none other than the Holy Spirit. At this particular place in the discourses Jesus is describing for his disciples the mission that the Holy Spirit will accomplish in the world after Jesus' departure to the Father, and a judgment against the ruler of this world is among the Spirit's works. And this reference to the role of the Holy Spirit constitutes Jesus' third assurance to his disciples.

Once again the limitations of the present study allow for only a brief analysis of Jesus' other assurances to his disciples concerning the coming of the Holy Spirit and concerning the support that the Holy Spirit will afford to them. Reference to the Holy Spirit occurs earlier within John's Gospel, but the Spirit's role is especially brought to the fore within the farewell discourses.[10] Jesus makes reference to the Spirit's role in four separate passages within the center section of the discourse (14:15-17; 14:25-26; 15:26-27; 16:7-15). Significantly in each of these passages Jesus uses the Greek word *paraklētos* in referring to the Holy Spirit. This word is usually translated either as "the Counselor" or as "the Paraclete."

It is of some moment that this Greek term only occurs five times within the entire New Testament (the present four instances and in 1 John 2:1). In terms of the present study it is particularly significant that, as used in other Greek sources, this word has a primarily juridical frame of reference.[11]

Jesus' initial statement concerning the Holy Spirit as Paraclete is simply that the Father will send *another* Paraclete to be with the disciples forever (14:15-17). Part of the work of the Paraclete will be to teach the disciples all things and especially to bring to remembrance all that Jesus himself has taught them (14:26). More precisely in terms of the juridical dimension, the Paraclete will bear witness to Jesus and will assist the disciples in making their own witness to Jesus (15:26-27).

Significantly, this particular promise of Jesus is made just after he has informed the disciples that they should expect persecution in the world (15:18-25).[12] Thus the Paraclete's role in this context can be likened to that performed by a "defense attorney." Subsequently, in a particularly rich passage in which Jesus consoles the disciples regarding his departure, he also alludes to the Paraclete's role in "convincing" or "convicting" the world and the ruler of the world (16:8-10). This passage has already been referred to; in contrast with the passage in chapter 15, the juridical role of the Spirit here is more akin to that of a "prosecuting attorney."[13]

If the continuing presence of the Holy Spirit on their behalf is thus an encouragement to his disciples to bear faithful witness in the world after his departure, Jesus extends a fourth kind of support to them by emphasizing that the final outcome of their witness is not in doubt. They will eventually prevail because Jesus himself has definitively overcome the world (16:33) and because the Father has given him "power over all flesh, to give eternal life to all whom thou has given him" (17:2).

Does Jesus not poignantly express this same idea in his final intercessory prayer, praying, "Father I desire that they also, whom thou hast given me, may be with me where I am, to behold my glory which thou hast given me in thy love for me before the foundation of the world" (17:24)? And again, "I made known to them thy name, and I will make it known, that the love with which thou hast loved me may be in them, and I in them" (17:26).

3. THE FAREWELL DISCOURSES IN THE CONTEXT
OF ROMAN PERSECUTION

It is not possible to establish definitively from presently existing data that some of John's readers were proximate to Roman persecution. More will be said about this subject in chapter eight below. However, for the sake of conceiving the maximum impact that Jesus' farewell addresses would have had in such circumstances, let it be assumed that at least some in John's audience were reading or hearing these chapters within a situation in which denunciations, Roman trials, and sentences of death were immediate realities.[14] This question then follows: Under such grave circumstances, what impact would the five elements just identified within Jesus' discourses have had upon John's readers?

A. Jesus' Prediction of Persecutions

As noted above, the words that John attributes to Jesus concerning persecution in chapters 15 and 16 primarily related to a future persecution that his disciples would experience at the hands of their religious adversaries. Nevertheless, it should now be observed that Jesus' words are phrased in such a way as to make them suitable resources for disciples whose persecution was occurring at the hands of *political* officials.

No extended discussion is required at this juncture for, *prima facie*, it seems clear that disciples facing Roman persecution would have consoled themselves with the thought that life-threatening persecution, *of one form or another,* had indeed been envisioned by Jesus. Still, with respect to the phenomenon of religious persecution, it is important to mention that the present thesis concerning "the application" of Jesus' words into situations of political persecution does not preclude that these same words could have been simultaneously valued by any of John's readers who were experiencing various kinds of persecution from religiously motivated adversaries.[15]

B. The Prediction of Apostasy

At this juncture reference is appropriately made to the contents of chapter three above and in particular to Pliny's measures against suspected Christians. It will be recalled that the desire to encourage apostasy was a major concern of Pliny's and literally an issue of life and death for those brought before him.

In particular two aspects of Pliny's investigations provide perspective on the issue of apostasy in early Christian history. The first is that Pliny discovered through his interrogations that some of those who had been denounced to him had apostasized over two years previously and some had even left their Christian faith twenty years earlier. Sparsely written, Pliny's report does not explain what factors motivated either of these groups to cease believing, nor does it provide any indication of the numbers involved or the impact that these departures had upon the Christian community or communities involved.

The second aspect regards Pliny's procedures with those who professed before him that they were active Christians. What was his intention in such cases? It was to pressure these Christians to apostasize! Pliny did this by repeatedly warning them that they would be executed if they persisted in their profession. He then gave them two additional chances to recant before ordering his soldiers to take them for execution. Again, his sparingly written report provides no indication as to the number of those so executed. Nor does it inform on a matter of considerable interest: whether any Christians actually recanted their faith in his presence.

With a view to assessing the impact of John's Gospel—recall John's thoroughgoing emphasis upon coming to and *remaining in* belief—these developments under Pliny are highly significant. For, as has been seen above, Jesus told his disciples to expect persecution and explained that one reason for his warning was to keep them from falling away under the impact of such persecution (16:1,4). Consider the starkness of the choices facing the Christians of Bithynia-Pontus. Those who had apostasized two years previously were ordered by Pliny to confirm their apostasy by giving reverence to the statue of Trajan and the images of the gods and by cursing the name of Christ. Presumably those who were convinced in their apostasy did so. But from the standpoint of the Gospel of John, at what a cost!

It can be inferred that the procedures used by Pliny to confirm the status of apostate Christians would also be followed in the cases of any active Christians who succumbed to Pliny's threats. In his presence they too would be expected to curse the name of Christ.

Viewed from the perspective of John's Gospel, the alternatives at such an imperial hearing could not possibly be starker: (a) to continue to proclaim allegiance to Jesus as sovereign Lord and suffer the loss of one's life in this world; (b) to be willing to curse Jesus' name publicly and thus cling to one's life in this world. Within John's Gospel there are indeed powerful dichotomies between belief and unbelief, between light and darkness, between life and death. One can hardly imagine situations better suited for illuminating these dichotomies and making them concrete than the real life episodes taking place before Pliny's tribunal.

C. Remaining Closely Bonded with Jesus

There is next the logically related issue of how Christian communities whose members were in danger of arrest might have prepared themselves to face Roman officials like Pliny. Here once again the extreme relevance of the christological material presented in the farewell discourses can be immediately recognized. For does it not emerge from Pliny's letter that christology is the central issue in such a Roman legal venue? For what are these Christians on trial for but *accusatio nominis*? They are accused for allegiance to the name of Jesus. And where shall these Christians, possessing John's Gospel, go for strengthening if not to the section of the Gospel that contains Jesus' words preparing his disciples for the period after his own return to the Father?

In this connection it is useful to try to imagine how a group of Christians facing Roman persecution might have tried to prepare for it. Several aspects might be regarded here, aspects pertaining to the composition and organization of a Christian community, to their practice with respect to the celebration of the Eucharist, their methods for receiving new members, and their patterns with respect to the catechesis of both new and long-standing members. Each of the foregoing aspects and others beside could plausibly be expected to influence the manner in which a given community might gird itself for the attack upon its existence and life that Roman persecution represented.

Inasmuch as the attack itself was fundamentally because of allegiance to Christ, so too would the preparation for withstanding this assault seemingly have to be christological. To be sure, the Gospel as a whole with its intense insistence upon Jesus' sovereign standing would provide substantive support for those Christians reading it, meditating upon it, and praying through it. Additionally, is it not easily imaginable that readings from Jesus' words in chapter 15 would have had a particularly saluatary impact? The image of Jesus as the vine and his disciples as the branches, and his teaching that the branches cannot bear fruit by themselves unless they abide in the vine—how powerfully might such images and words have been proclaimed in an assembly of those whose very lives were to be decided by whether they chose to *remain* in Jesus.

In the previous section reference has already been made to the concept of being a friend of Jesus as expressed in chapter 15 of the Gospel and the concept of being a friend of Caesar that is delineated in chapter 19. Here it suffices merely to recall that juxtaposition and to suggest that the prayer and encouragement of a gathered Christian community to all of its members might well have been to stand firm as a "friend of Jesus" whatever the cost of doing so. Pliny formulated his test for apostates in precisely these alternative terms: to curse the name of Christ and revere the image of Caesar. In encouraging one another, might not Christians familiar with John's Gospel have framed their encouragement in terms no less stark: Better to be the friend of Jesus than the friend of Pliny's Caesar? Better to lay down one's life as a friend of Jesus than to compromise with Pliny for "friendship" with Trajan.

In essence, what is being suggested here is that persecuted Christians in Bithynia-Pontus and elsewhere could have scarcely found a better "christological shield" with which to withstand persecution than the words and images of Jesus present in John's farewell chapters. Beyond the images just cited, other elements of these discourses could also conceivably have had a strong resonance among those gathered in Jesus' name. Indeed, the flowing, undulating character of the discourses as a whole can be appreciated anew in reference to such a context. As John portrays it, Jesus' farewell introduces important images and concepts with an almost wavelike effect. Those under threat of persecution may well have spent extended periods of time together. Passages from the discourses could conceivably have been read publicly and then followed with periods for personal meditation. Intervals for public prayer and public exhortation may also have been blended into the time of assembly.

D. Love for One Another

At this point the theme of Jesus' disciples' love for one another appropriately comes forward for consideration. It is precisely love *for one another* that Jesus emphasizes in the farewell discourses, and thus it is important to reflect about the meaning that such a "restricted" commandment[16] would have possessed in the circumstances of persecution.

Above all, the reality of a persecution against a provincial Christian community introduces the factor of decision. Faced with a persecution akin to that of Pliny, what counts above all in terms of the life of a Christian community is that its members have the courage to stand firm and give steady witness to their belief in Jesus. It is a time for those who have already come to belief in Jesus to express a love that may require the laying down of their lives for him.

Yet clearly to prepare for such a momentous step, if there is time to prepare, it is to the interest of the community members to draw together for intense mutual encouragement. In other circumstances Christians can easily be imagined evangelizing in the public places of towns and cities. With the advent of persecution, though, there is almost inevitably a need for a closing of ranks in an effort to defend against this threat and to withstand it. This very image of a community gathered together in love and intimacy during a time of persecution is in fact almost the very image provided in John's description of Jesus' presence with his disciples under the circumstances of his approaching "hour."

This image of the community under persecution drawing more intensely together in love is closely tied to the previously suggested considerations about the way in which a persecuted community would attempt to strengthen the personal allegiance of its individual members to Jesus. In the crucible of life-threatening and community-threatening persecution there would not be a clear distinction between one activity and the other. Rather much is occurring within a short interval, and many facets of Jesus' legacy are being adverted to simultaneously.

E. Other Forms of Assurance

Similarly, the other words with which Jesus provides assurances and consolation in his final discourses may well have been appropriated by a persecuted community in a somewhat "random" way. The preceding section of this chapter identified four kinds of instruction from Jesus that were intended to provide his disciples with encouragement for the period after his departure: (1) that his departure fulfills the Father's plan and will benefit the disciples; (2) that despite Satan's continuing presence, Jesus' disciples will be preserved from "the evil one"; (3) that the Paraclete will come; and (4) that the final outcome of his followers' witness is not in doubt. It is now appropriate to conceptualize the meaning, at least with broad strokes, that these four encouraging assurances would have held for a persecuted community meditating and praying over them.

Extended reflections might be written in explicating the intense consolation that Christians proximate to the loss of their lives for Jesus would have derived from the following reassuring words:

> Let not your hearts be troubled; believe in God, believe also in me. In my Father's house are many rooms; if it were not so, would I have told you that I go to prepare a place for you? And when I go and prepare a place for you, I will come again and will take you to myself, that where I am you may be also (14:1-3).

For a time Jesus' disciples would have to face persecution. And then Jesus would come for them. And bring them to his Father's house in which there are, *for them*, many rooms. As mentioned previously, this first element of Jesus' encouragement is complemented strongly by the fourth element. And, accordingly, further reflection upon the significant meaning contained in this passage is appropriately delayed until the fourth aspect is considered below.

It can be inferred from a careful consideration of Pliny's reports to Trajan that the Christians of his region not only faced martyrdom but also two concomitant evils: betrayal by an informer and the threat of apostasy. Whether Pliny's informer was someone centrally involved in the life of the Christian community or someone at its edges is not revealed in the letter. However, even if the secret informer was only someone on the edges of Christian life, the evil in this secret denunciation is still horrendous. From the perspective of those committed to give their lives for Jesus there is also horrendous evil in the conduct of those former Christians who now blithely come forward to revere the image of the emperor and to revile the name of Jesus. In addition, there is manifest evil residing in the fact that dedicated Christians are now undergoing persecution. Why is such evil befalling them merely because they have professed belief in Jesus?

How were Pliny's Christians and others in comparable circumstances to gain perspective on these evils befalling them and their loved ones? As they sought to understand this evil and explain it, a second aspect contained in Jesus' assurances would have been extremely helpful to them. For the important reality that would have become clear to them as they pondered his assurances was this: These evils were due in part to the continuing presence in the world of *the evil one*, Satan, "the ruler of this world."

Satan thus does have influence in the situation of the Christians who are subject to Pliny. Yet even more important, as is also clear from Jesus' discourse, Satan's influence will not be definitive in the disciples' situation any more than it was definitive in Jesus' situation. Satan did enter into Judas at the time of the supper and Judas did betray Jesus by informing and conspiring against him. And was there not apostasy in the denials of Jesus by Peter? Yet Jesus himself stated, just after adverting to the fact that the ruler of this world was approaching, *"He has no power over me"* (14:30b). And finally Jesus himself expressly prayed for his disciple in the following way: "I do not pray that thou shouldst take them out of the world, but that thou shouldst *keep them from the evil one"* (17:15).

Later disciples facing the evils of betrayal, apostasy, and persecution unto death thus have assurances from Jesus to assist them and encourage them. Jesus himself has passed through these evils to a life beyond them. Still further, he promised the Paraclete, the Holy Spirit, to them as a direct assistance to them in facing these sufferings. This is the third element of Jesus' farewell assurances to be considered.

To be noted is that in Jesus' words the Paraclete has a role to play in assisting the disciples in their own witness and also a role to play in *convincing* or *convicting* "the ruler of this world." In trial situations before Pliny and his counterparts, the Holy Spirit will aid Jesus' believing disciples in preparing their testimony and then in making it with full fidelity. Jesus' disciples, his friends, are thus not left to their own resources. In a mysterious manner, not fully explained, the Holy Spirit will be present to them as a kind of "defense attorney" to help them maintain and confess their belief.

Similarly, the Paraclete's work in subjecting "the world" and "the ruler of this world" to judgment is not fully explained. Yet for those pondering them, Jesus' words are clear enough to provide consolation and strength. For it is not that the evil of the world and the evil perpetrated by Satan in influencing betrayal, apostasy, and sentences of death are to go unrequited. There will be, in some definitive yet unspecified fashion, a judgment against the evil of this world and against its "ruler."

This too is assurance; this too is encouragement for Christian communities threatened by and beleaguered by the evil of persecution. There remains now only to treat the subject area of the final outcome for those who are faithful. This fourth area of encouragement is, as has been remarked, akin to the first area. Like the first area it has to do with the larger framework of the world "above," which is operative over and beyond the persecuted disciples' immediate circumstances. It is the area of encouragement that has to do with Jesus' ultimate victory and with life everlasting.

In concrete circumstances of betrayal and apostasies and death sentences, believing Christians must not lose sight of or be shaken from the truth that, in the end, it is Jesus who is sovereign. It is not any informer who speaks the final word. It is not the one who apostasizes and makes obeisance to the emperor who speaks the final word. Nor is it the Roman governor who orders the death of Jesus' disciples who speaks the final word. Not any of these but only Jesus, who has overcome all evil, is authorized by the Father to speak the final word. And what is Jesus' final sovereign word? There is hardly a more definitive pronouncement of his on this point than that which occurs in John 16:33b: "I have overcome the world."

And thus the image of Jesus excercising ultimate sovereignty beyond any word, any judgment, that has been spoken against his faithful disciples! What response will the Father give when Jesus' work is complete? Earlier it was alluded to that Jesus would come for his faithful disciples and bring them to his Father's house. In a slightly different way this same outcome is expressed in Jesus' solemn concluding prayer to the Father (17:2). There he indicates that the disciples' final reality will be nothing less than life everlasting: "... since thou hast given him power over all flesh, to give eternal life to all whom thou hast given him."[17]

7

John 20-21 and Readers in Roman Surroundings

Two chapters of John's Gospel that are highly relevant to the concerns of this study have yet to be expressly considered. Accordingly, the present chapter takes up the rich material contained in John 20 and John 21 and seeks to assess its potential impact for Christians living under the aegis of Roman rule.

1. JOHN 21 AND THE BODY OF JOHN'S GOSPEL

In chapter one of this study a number of considerations relative to the text and authorship of John's Gospel were set forth. At the outset of the present chapter dealing with the ending of John's Gospel, it is appropriate that attention again be directed to this general subject area.

Especially because of the fact that the final verses of John 20 can be regarded as a highly appropriate conclusion for John's narrative, the precise relationship between John 21 and the preceding twenty chapters is a disputed issue within Johannine studies.[1] Before referring again to a criterion that has a decisive influence upon the approach followed in the present study, it is well to indicate several of the theories concerning the origin and function of chapter 21. The following discussion is by no means exhaustive of the possibilities.

First, it is conceivable that the principal writer of the Gospel originally envisioned a work of twenty chapters and consciously intended Thomas' dramatic confession as his final scene and 20:30-31 as his concluding author's note. Then, however, after an interval, this writer returned to the manuscript and added the material now comprising chapter 21 as an appendix or epilogue. This appendix is itself ended by the author's note of 21:24-25.

Second, it is conceivable that the principal writer of the Gospel was specifically concerned to indicate the course of discipleship to which Peter and the beloved disciple were called and thus always envisioned chapter 21 as an integral part of the Gospel. However, within this twenty-one chapter framework, Thomas' confession was still consciously intended to serve as a culminating affirmation of Jesus' true identity.

A third conceivable interpretation that is more complex envisions the involvement of one or more persons beyond the *initial* writer or writers of the Gospel. In one variation of this interpretation, a later writer-editor took responsibility for confirming, revising, and supplementing the work of a predecessor or predecessors who were largely responsible for the contents of chapters 1-20. This later writer-editor's work is also to be noted in the addition of the passages now comprising chapter 21. The material included in this chapter was thus not known by, or at least was not included by, the initial writer or writers.

In light of these three possibilities and others besides,[2] what basic approach does the present study follow in analyzing the "ending" of John's Gospel? There is one crucial factor, already alluded to in chapter one of this study that facilitates forward movement. It is this: that John 21 is included in all of the presently existing ancient manuscripts and thus almost certainly circulated in the early Christian communities as integrally related to the preceding chapters of the Gospel![3]

What this means, practically speaking, is that any study seeking to assess the impact of the Gospel of John, *as it circulated*,[4] is not merely authorized but is actually mandated to treat the material contained in John 21. This, in fact, was the rationale for including material from John 21 in the analysis of Jesus as Lord that was made in chapter four above. And, accordingly, section three below will analyze additional relevant material from this chapter.

2. KEY ELEMENTS OF CHAPTER 20

In this section and in section three there is a certain correspondence between the treatment accorded to John 20 and that accorded to John 21. The resurrection appearances of Jesus in both chapters will be considered in broad terms, an important passage from within each chapter will be considered in some detail, and finally the "author's note" at the end of each of these chapters will be analyzed. Again, it is worth noting that the treatment to be accorded to these two chapters is far from exhaustive. Only the briefest reference to one of the extended commentaries of John's Gospel will indicate that there is much within these two chapters that is scarcely being touched upon here.

It is well to begin this analysis with a consideration of Jesus' transformed existence in his encounter with Mary Magdalene. John indicates that she was the first to visit the tomb and to see that the stone had been rolled away (20:1). As previously indicated in chapter four above, Mary Magdalene was also the first disciple to whom Jesus appeared. Yet what are Jesus' exact movements and characteristics at the time of these events? John describes only that Mary Magdalene saw Jesus standing near the tomb without recognizing him at first. And as to how Jesus departed from her, the narrative is altogether silent. Nevertheless, it is evident from John's overall description of this encounter (20:14-17) that, in his new identity, Jesus is no longer subject to the constraints of space and time.

This conclusion is confirmed by John's report of the risen Jesus' next appearance (20:19-22). His disciples were gathered in a room whose doors are securely locked, yet Jesus suddenly "came" (*ēlthen*) and stood among them. John's report clearly emphasizes that it was Jesus and none other, for Jesus expressly shows them his hands and sides (20:26-27). He twice extends a greeting of peace to them, commissions them as the Father has sent him, imparts the Holy Spirit, and gives them the specific authority for forgiving sins (20:19-23).

Again John does not explicitly relate how Jesus departed from the disciples on this occasion, yet by now his readers are oriented to the fact that the risen Jesus moves in a mysterious fashion. John's description of Jesus' appearance eight days later, this time with Thomas present, is in the same vein. The doors were shut but Jesus came and stood among them extending the greeting of peace (20:26). He then offered Thomas the opportunity to inspect the reality of his body now amazingly transformed. Thomas was then invited to place his finger and his hand where the marks of crucifixion remained (20:27).

This episode with Thomas and particularly Thomas' reply represent the passage of chapter 20 that is of extraordinary importance within the perspective of the present study. Notwithstanding the commitment of the present study to appreciate fully the contents of chapter 21, a strong case can still be made that John regards Jesus' encounter with Thomas as the culminating scene of the body of the Gospel. Jesus' words within this passage themselves also afford support for such an interpretation.[5] He states as his motivation for extending such a dramatic invitation that Thomas "not be faithless but believing" (20:27b). And then, in a majestic comment upon Thomas' confession, he states, "Have you believed because you have seen me? Blessed are those who have not seen and yet believe" (20:29).

In and of itself Thomas' memorable confession of belief and allegiance supports the interpretation that this is indeed to be regarded as the Gospel's culminating scene. Without belaboring the analysis made previously in chapter four on this point, it can be simply stated here that no more illustrious acclaim is given to Jesus within the Fourth Gospel than Thomas' "my Lord and my God." The effect of such a scene, especially when followed by the author's solemn statement concerning his purpose in writing, is to provide readers of the Gospel with a sense of closure and satisfaction.

Further, it can also be seen that such a "high" closing comports well with the first statement made in the Gospel prologue about Jesus' identity.[6] For John wrote at the end of his very first verse that "the Word was God."

In effect, then, the evangelist can be seen to fashion a powerful "inclusion" from 1:1 to 20:28 of the Gospel. Jesus is described as being of the essence of God at the outset of the Gospel and then, fully twenty chapters later, one of his disciples comes to believe in him fully and affirms him loftily as "my Lord and my God."

Specifically regarding John's author's note in 20:30-31, it is again the case that virtually every phrase used by the evangelist is rich with meaning. In verse 30 and verse 31a John explains that the signs of Jesus he has detailed within the Gospel have been selected from a still larger body of signs that Jesus performed in the presence of the disciples. Then in his final verse John explicitly indicates two of his fundamental purposes in writing his work: (a) that his readers may believe, and (b) that they may have life.

It is important to recognize the close relationship between these two expressed purposes. "That you may believe" is itself a fundamental statement about the meaning of the Gospel and John's intention in authoring it.[7] Yet the consequence of believing is itself of extreme importance for John; this consequence is that his readers have eternal life. The one purpose thus involves the other, for to have eternal life cannot be separated from believing.

The other elements that John includes within his author's note must also be carefully considered. What are these elements? John refers to Jesus with the extended phrase, "the Christ, the Son of God." This title may well have delineated an aspect of Jesus' sovereignty that was particularly meaningful to Jewish readers of the Gospel (that Jesus is the Christ, the long-awaited Messiah) and an aspect that would have been especially meaningful for those readers from a Gentile background (that Jesus is the exalted Son of God). Whatever the other dimensions of meaning present in this title, what is unmistakably clear is that the Jesus to whom John was summoning his readers is a Jesus whose sovereign status is unsurpassed. In addition, John avers that it is because they are "in his name" that those who believe in Jesus have eternal life. This phrase thus marks the conclusion of his author's note. John has set forth the Gospel so that, believing, his readers may have life *in his name*.[8]

3. KEY ELEMENTS OF CHAPTER 21

Recognizing that there are many significant features in the first seventeen verses of John 21,[9] the first paragraphs of this section will concentrate attention upon Jesus' sovereignty and his special affirmation of Peter. Obviously, the aspect of Jesus' sovereignty does not represent the breaking of new ground within the Gospel. In contrast, the role that is described for Peter in these verses does represent a substantially new development within John's narrative and is one that possesses several dimensions of meaning.

According to John 21, Jesus' third appearance in risen form takes place not in Jerusalem or Judea but in Galilee at the edge of the Sea of Tiberias. Significantly, when Jesus appears on the beach, these seven disciples are offshore in a fishing boat: Peter, Thomas, Nathaniel, the sons of Zebedee, and the two other disciples (21:2-3). As with Mary Magdalene in the previous chapter, at first they do not recognize him (21:4). However, after they follow his instructions and catch a great quantity of fish, the beloved disciple exclaims to Peter that it is the Lord—with the result that Peter springs naked into the sea making his way to Jesus as quickly as possible (21:5-8).

Jesus' full sovereignty is thus attested to again by his power to appear to his disciples and instruct them to such a bountiful catch of fish. That this transformed figure is indeed Jesus is underscored by John's statement that *"Jesus* came and took the bread and gave it to them and so with the fish" (21:13; italics added). Jesus, the one denied by Peter, is thus the one who begins to speak with Peter after this breakfast.

The risen Jesus' three questions to Peter in this setting are well known, and that Peter's three affirmations of love correspond to his three denials of Jesus after his arrest (18:17,25,27) is also well recognized. Similarly enhanced by a threefold repetition is the pastoral commission that Jesus gives to Peter: "Feed my lambs ... Tend my sheep ... Feed my sheep." When this passage (21:15-17) is regarded as a whole from the standpoint of the present study, two additional features come to the fore. First, Jesus' sovereign powers are again witnessed to. There are several indications of this feature but it is especially prominent in Peter's final poignant response to Jesus: "Lord, you know *everything*: you know that I love you" (21:17; italics added).

The second feature concerns Peter himself. Jesus' threefold affirmation of him comes within the context of preceding verses in which Peter has been portrayed taking three initiatives: It was Peter's decision to go fishing in the first place (21:2); he is the one who immediately sprang into the water when the beloved disciple recognized Jesus on the shore; and Peter, identified by name, is the disciple who hauled the net filled with fish ashore once the boat had beached (21:11).

Peter is thus prominently portrayed in the first episodes of chapter 21.[10] And, as will now be seen, this pattern continues in the next episode involving Peter, the beloved disciple, and Jesus. Exactly at which point in the narrative the setting changes from a situation in which the other disciples are present to one in which Jesus, Peter, and the beloved disciple seem to walk alone along the beach cannot be determined precisely. Nevertheless, the slight blurring with respect to venue scarcely diminishes the highly significant comment Jesus makes to Peter in this second setting and the remarkable conversation the two of them then shared.

After his third commission to Peter, Jesus' next reported words to him are the following:

Truly, truly, I say to you, when you were young, you girded yourself and walked where you would; but when you are old, you will stretch out your hands, and another will gird you and carry you where you do not wish to go (21:18).

Taken apart from the author's explanatory comment in the following verse, these words are somewhat allusive. "You will stretch out your hands and another will gird you" is regarded by many commentators as a reference to crucifixion.[11] Similarly, the following clause, "and carry you where you do not wish to go," can also be readily interpreted as emphasizing the involuntary aspect of death by crucifixion. That this is indeed the understanding intended is established definitely by John's own parenthetical note in the verse following:

This he said to show by what death he was to glorify God (21:19a).[12]

At this juncture the evangelist reports Jesus addressing a remarkable command to Peter. This command is expressed in just two words (21:19b): "Follow me."[13] Given that Jesus' own passion and glorification have just occurred and given that Jesus has just indicated that martyrdom lies ahead for Peter these latter words must almost certainly be regarded as bidding Peter to accept the course that Jesus has identified for him. These words also serve as a definite encouragement to Peter. In effect, the risen Jesus, having passed through his own trial and crucifixion, now imparts to the disciple he has just restored that he (Peter) must follow Jesus along Jesus' own course to glory.

In its own right the conversation that occurs next is also extremely significant for the perspective that it sheds upon Peter, upon Peter's martyrdom, and upon the beloved disciple's own life course. This conversation is also highly remarkable given the usually exalted form of Jesus' speech within John's Gospel, for Peter is shown to be walking and speaking with Jesus in a manner that is characterized by extraordinary familiarity.[14] In 21:20 John portrays Peter walking beside Jesus with the beloved disciple following a little behind. Having just heard Jesus' words regarding his own future, Peter then asks Jesus about the future course of the beloved disciple's life (21:21b): "Lord, what about this man?" Jesus' response to this query is so significant that it is appropriate to cite it in full before proceeding to comment upon its several dimensions:

Jesus said to him, "If it is my will that he remain until I come, what is that to you? Follow me!" (21:22).

A first point to be noticed is that in this passage (as well as in several previous passages), the disciple referred to as the beloved disciple is portrayed in a highly positive fashion.[15] In this episode the beloved disciple is once again in close proximity to Jesus, and now Jesus strikingly foretells his personal future, indicating that he will not experience martyrdom but will rather *"remain* until I come." Several issues pertaining to this disciple's identity and fate are significant and deservedly have received extended treatment within the scholarly literature.[16] However, at the present juncture of this study the focus must be upon the fact that the beloved disciple's following of Jesus will not involve martyrdom.

Second, the phrasing of Jesus' words is such as to tender a gentle rebuke to Peter. In the closeness and ease of his own relationship with Jesus, he has been emboldened to inquire regarding the life course of another disciple. Jesus answers this intrusive inquiry, but after doing so he adds the gentle reminder, " . . . what is that to you?" Having thus cautioned Peter against undue concern over another's calling, Jesus then explicitly reemphasizes to Peter that *his* call is precisely to follow Jesus through a martyr's death. "Follow me!" is Jesus' imperative at this point (21:22b).[17] Thus he dramatically repeats the command he gave Peter three verses earlier, using essentially the same words but now more emphatically.

The verses that then follow to conclude this chapter can be regarded as an author's note comparable to that which follows the Thomas passage of chapter 20. This second note attests to the important role of the beloved disciple in the composition of the Gospel and thus provides a closing in which the contributions of these two figures, Peter and the beloved disciple, are both in the reader's view.[18] The final verse of this second author's note can itself be regarded as a reprise of the majestic verses that form the conclusion of the note in chapter 20.[19] For purposes of comparison these two closing sentences are now presented:

Now Jesus did many other signs in the presence of the disciples, which are not written in this book; but these are written that you may believe that Jesus is the Christ, the Son of God, and that believing you may have life in his name (20:30-31).

But there are also many other things which Jesus did; were every one of them to be written, I suppose that the world itself could not contain the books that would be written (21:25).

4. JOHN 20-21 AND READERS IN A ROMAN CONTEXT

The principal task of the present section is to reflect upon the foregoing material of John 20 and John 21 from the presumed situation of readers who faced Roman imperial claims and possibly Roman persecution as well. Structurally the present section thus corresponds with sections 6.1 and 6.3 in the preceding chapter. It will be recalled that in those two sections assessments were made concerning the implications of Jesus' sovereignty at his Roman trial and concerning the implications of the assurances Jesus imparted in his farewell discourses.

John's reports concerning Jesus' first two resurrection appearances, to

Mary Magdalene on Easter morning and to the disciples on Easter evening, testify both to his sovereignty over death and to his passage beyond the laws of space and time. Jesus' powers are now manifestly far beyond those of any earthly ruler or authority. There is additional cause, therefore, for John's readers to give belief and allegiance to him and to trust fully in his ability to bring them to "my Father and your Father, to my God and your God."

John's narrative describing Jesus' appearance to Thomas would have constituted an even more powerful resource for his readers when they were faced with questions of allegiance engendered by the Roman authorities. In such a setting the alternatives are likely to be quite stark. Equally stark is the alternative with which the risen Jesus confronts Thomas. To continue as Jesus' disciple Thomas has to move decisively to belief: "Do not be faithless . . . but believing."

Within situations in which allegiance was controverted, there was also an unsurpassed resource for John's readers in Thomas' full, resounding acclamation, "My Lord and my God." Depending upon various factors, John's readers might conceivably affirm to each other that it was now time to make Thomas' words their own. Convinced in their hearts that Thomas' words were true, they might now mutually encourage one another to speak these same words publicly.[20]

Blessed are these later disciples who came to such belief and remained firm in it. For did not Jesus himself respond to Thomas that blessed indeed are those who have not had the benefit of seeing him but yet believe? Such is the situation of John's readers. They have not seen Jesus yet they continue to believe even in the face of ominous imperial claims. Some of them may even be facing martyrdom as a consequence of their belief.

As considered above, John's author's note at the end of chapter 20 emphasizes Jesus' majestic status, referring to him as "Christ" and "Son of God." It also reminds readers of the Gospel that other sovereign signs were worked by Jesus in the presence of his disciples. And, significantly, the final verse of this note stresses the connection between belief in Jesus and life everlasting. Once again the rich meaning that such fundamental themes would have had for Christians facing Roman claims and challenges can hardly be exaggerated. It is perhaps appropriate to suggest that still further attention be focused upon the meaning of John's last three words within his already richly filled final sentence.

As a qualifying phrase to his exhortation that those continuing in belief will have eternal life, John appends the words "in his name" (*en tō onomati autou*). These words were noted in section one of this chapter but not discussed with reference to their potentially energy-imparting impact upon any readers who faced a situation comparable to that faced by the Christians of Bithynia-Pontus hailed before Pliny's tribunal. Even Christians not directly threatened by overt persecution could well have reflected upon this phrase with profit. Yet for any of John's readers contending with the likes of Pliny, the power contained within these words is incontrovertibly greater.

Why, specifically, is the concept of the name of Christ so potentially rich in meaning for Christians subject to trial by Roman officials like Pliny? First, it should be recalled that the correspondence between Pliny and Trajan established that Christians were liable to death simply "for the name," that is, simply because they identified themselves with the name of Christ. The name of Christ, then, was a *capital offense.*

Second, under Pliny's trial procedures, the name of Christ was a *test.* For it was by means of their attitude toward this name that Pliny determined who of those before him were really Christians. Strikingly, for apostate Christians the test is the means whereby they preserve their lives in this world. Whatever their previous level of commitment, they are willing now (for some, perhaps because of extreme duress) to curse the name of Christ. And by doing so they are exculpated in Pliny's eyes. They leave his tribunal free to resume their daily lives.

In contrast, although but a few words were asked of them, the persevering Christians who stood before Pliny were literally a world away from uttering them. Facing pressure to curse the name of Christ, they believed only this: *in his name* was life that was true and eternal. They surely knew that, faced with their perseverance, Pliny would order their execution. Yet more fundamentally did they believe that, by remaining firm in *his* name, they would enter upon a life unending.

How poignant and how powerful would the final words of the author's note thus appear to any of John's readers who were involved in Roman trials in which the name of Christ was both the offense in question and the test to be used to verify the offense. Even absent a situation of immediate persecution, the clear proclamation of Jesus' sovereignty in John's concluding sentence was something that readers could ponder in reference to the challenges posed by the imperial cult. This same point regarding the risen Jesus' sovereignty and the cult of the Roman emperors is also a valid one with respect to the material that John went on to present in chapter 21.

Again, in considering the potential of the material contained in John 21 for influencing readers living under Roman rule, it must be emphasized that this chapter was always attached to the rest of the Gospel. And thus for the first recipients of John's work these passages were part and parcel of a single authorized document.

John's account of Jesus' appearance to the disciples at the Sea of Tiberias thus possessed the full potential for reinforcing his previous passages concerning Jesus' transformed sovereign status and his continuing clairvoyant knowledge. In addition, there are two descriptions within chapter 21 that would have presumably provided John's readers with new information pertaining to the realities of Roman rule. These descriptions pertain to the life courses of two of Jesus' leading disciples, Peter and the beloved disciple.

In the preceding section of this study the various aspects of Peter's prominent position within chapter 21 were delineated. The risen Jesus provides Peter with the opportunity for redeeming his previous denials, dramatically entrusts him with major pastoral responsibility, and then summons him to a course of discipleship involving martyrdom. Certainly this last aspect, the aspect of Peter's martyrdom, would have possessed the highest significance for John's readers as they sought to determine the implications of their Christian identity within a Roman context.

It is worth dwelling for a moment upon the fact that Peter's death will be death by Roman crucifixion. In effect, what this means is that John's readers now came face to face with the realities that Jesus, their sovereign Lord, and Peter, one of his closest disciples, *both* received a sentence of death from Roman officials! Who then among these readers will not have cause to reflect about the possible outcome of their own lives under Roman rule? Already before them from the farewell discourses were Jesus' predictions regarding persecution and the danger of apostasy. Now John's readers are led to reflect further regarding their own (Roman) circumstances as a result of Jesus' specific prediction concerning a martyr's death for Peter. Might not events conceivably turn in such a way that they themselves would also face death for their belief in Jesus?[21]

That Peter had been portrayed within the Gospel as a highly prominent disciple of Jesus may also have been significant for John's readers as they pondered his crucifixion. As noted above, Jesus had entrusted him with an extraordinary pastoral commission before indicating his manner of death to him. Might not John's readers have accordingly reflected that some of those called to pastoral service within the Christian community could also be called to martyrdom? This consideration possesses a two-edged significance; it has implications for the communities themselves and for those individuals serving in pastoral capacities within Christian communities.

A further reflection concerning the meaning of Jesus' words to Peter is that they do not envision martyrdom as a tragedy. Rather, Peter's death, a martyr's death, is a calling: "Follow me" (21:19). Any of John's readers facing martyrdom would have derived consolation from this point. And this idea would also have been profoundly consoling to close friends of the martyrs and to the communities of faith from which they were uprooted. In effect, John's Gospel expresses a lofty ideal for its readers: Peter's death on a Roman cross is a call from Jesus, their sovereign Lord, to share the death and glorification that he himself had experienced.

If a word about Peter's life course would have been greatly appreciated by John's readers, the evangelist's following reports about the beloved disciple would hardly have been less valuable to them. This is particularly so because such startling information is imparted at the end of chapter 21 — that the beloved disciple's testimony and writing have provided the basis for this Gospel!

It would require moving too far afield to discuss at this point the full implications of verse 21:24 for the subject of the Gospel's authorship. How-

ever, regardless of whether this verse attributes sole authorship to him, it
certainly ascribes to the beloved disciple a contribution that is of the highest
magnitude.[22] For this reason John's statement is appropriately cited in its
entirety: "This is the disciple who is bearing witness to these things, and
who has written these things, and we know that his testimony is true"
(21:24).

What implications flow from the fact that such a privileged role in the
preparation of the Gospel is indicated for the beloved disciple? From the
perspective of the present study, it is of critical significance that the beloved
disciple, unlike Peter, is *not* called to martyrdom. Rather, as indicated
above, Jesus' word to Peter concerning the beloved disciple is that he will
remain until the time of Jesus' coming.

In and of itself this dominical statement would have been sufficient to
enable readers of the Gospel to infer that only some of Jesus' disciples
were called to give their lives as martyrs. The beloved disciple, whose closeness to Jesus was highly remarkable, was not called by Jesus to this form
of witness. And yet how very fruitful was the beloved disciple's own particular calling. It was so fruitful as to make possible the existence of the
Gospel itself!

The readers of John 21 are thus left with memorable and instructive
images regarding two distinct forms of discipleship. On the one hand is the
image of Peter, who has a definite calling to follow Jesus through crucifixion; on the other hand is the image of the beloved disciple, whose call was
to *remain* and whose "bearing witness" had resulted in the formulation of
the Gospel.

Given that both were envisioned by the risen Jesus, these two expressions
of discipleship could scarcely be regarded as anything other than complementary.[23] And both had the potential for resulting in much fruit. Accordingly, any Christians within John's readership who were called to give their
lives through crucifixion and other forms of Roman execution should persevere in this calling without worrying over the fate of other disciples (recall
Jesus' gentle admonition to Peter in 21:22). Revering the witness of these
martyrs but at the same time secure in the legitimacy of their own call,
those asked by Jesus to *remain* should respond faithfully and seek to bear
appropriate fruit just as the beloved disciple had.

With such powerful inspiring images of complementary faithful discipleship does John's account thus close. And surely this imaging of Peter and
the beloved disciple comports extremely well with the image of Thomas
that is the climax of John 20. For John's readers in various circumstances
within the empire, there was indeed much to be pondered in the respective
responses of these three: Thomas, Peter, and the beloved disciple.

8

The Purposes of the Gospel of John

It is now time to draw together the results of the analyses made in the preceding chapters of this study with a view to addressing the issue of John's purposes in writing. The first sentence of this study asserted that John was concerned to present elements and themes that were significant for Christians facing Roman imperial claims and for any who faced Roman persecution. This thesis concerning one of John's purposes will now be argued systematically and brief attention will also be given to several of John's other presumed purposes in setting forth his Gospel.

1. JOHN'S CONSCIOUSNESS OF ROMAN REALITIES

Given the tendency for elements and themes pertaining to Roman realities to be neglected by commentaries on the Gospel of John, it is desirable to step back and take time for a moment or two in order to "image" John within his Roman circumstances. For, as indicated at the outset of the present study, wherever John was actually based, it is unassailable that he was located somewhere within the confines of the Roman empire.

Obviously there are numerous questions that might be formulated in an effort to stimulate imagination about John's circumstances and their potential impact upon him. To place two very basic questions that are germane to this study, it may be asked first whether John was knowledgeable regarding the administrative structure of the empire. And second, did John understand the fundamental objectives and priorities of Roman officials?

The answers to such questions follow easily. For how could John as a person of undoubted insight and sensitivity not have been aware of these fundamental features of his situation? Nevertheless, such rudimentary questions are useful as the entry point toward further reflections concerning John's consciousness of Roman realities. In effect, both of these questions were answered on an *a priori* basis without reference to any item that John published and without reference to anything that has been written about John's outlook by other ancient writers.

Let it now be asked whether John knew about the circumstances of the Jewish Tax and how it was administered. Here again, on an *a priori* basis, an affirmative answer can be given. For given the exaction of the tax everywhere that Jews were located and given the controversy surrounding it, how could John not have been aware of it? If he was informed concerning this tax, would this awareness not also have engendered reflections on his part about the various demands of the Roman state? For even if this tax was not demanded of John and his readers, their close proximity and/or affinity with Jews who were so constrained must surely have occasioned reflection about the claims of the Roman state vis-à-vis religious groups.

To what degree was John informed concerning the developing cult of the Roman emperors? To frame this question is now to approach one of the two areas that are of primary concern within the present work. As was indicated in chapter two, a comprehensive analysis of the imperial cult is beyond the boundaries of this study. Yet in different settings within the empire this cult was extensively practiced and fostered. And it is now appropriate to consider whether John was familiar with the various practices that were initiated by the emperors themselves, by their most zealous admirers, and by other proponents of the Roman system of deities.

At this stage the deductive procedure followed for the preceding questions can be complemented and thereby strengthened. Because he was a literate and reflective Christian, John would almost certainly have been knowledgeable regarding some features of the imperial cult. However, in addition to this deduction, there is also a basis for concluding John's familiarity with aspects of the imperial cult because of several references that are contained within his text. The presence of the titles "Lord," "Lord and God," and "Savior of the world," and the presence of the concept "friend of Caesar," all tend to indicate that John knew of these honorifics in their Roman setting and knew of the claims associated with them.

In the third section below more than this will be argued for on the basis of the *precise way* in which these titles are actually positioned within John's account. However, their very presence within John's final text offers strong support for the judgment that John's personal awareness of things Roman extended to at least certain features of the imperial cult as well.

But was John knowledgeable regarding Roman measures against Christains that resulted in their martyrdom? Here the matter is extremely complex due to significant uncertainties regarding chronology. On the one hand, as noted in chapter six, there is uncertainty regarding the dates at which the Roman hostility toward the Christian movement first began to manifest itself. When did Christians first find themselves before Roman tribunals? When did they first find themselves executed on the orders of Roman officials? On the other hand, as indicated in chapter one, there is a great range in scholarly opinion concerning the dates for John's Gospel.

Given these complexities with respect to chronology, etc., no easy initial assumptions can be made concerning John's knowledge about any forms of

Roman persecution. Nevertheless, there is one Gospel passage that seemingly does indicate his consciousness regarding at least one Christian's Roman martyrdom. And significantly the disciple mentioned in this passage is Peter, one of the two foremost disciples. The passage in question is John 21:18-19, the passage containing Jesus' prediction of Peter's death by crucifixion.

It is thus the case that John's knowledge of Christian martyrdom is primarily being deduced from the material of John 21:18-19. In essence, it is being argued that John would not have included this passage if Peter or other Christians before Peter had not already suffered martyrdom. Admittedly there is a slim possibility that this may not have been the situation and that John included this passage for other reasons. However, when the present passage's apparent interest in Christian martyrdom is supplemented by numerous other passages within the Gospel that pertain to Christian persecution more or less directly, it seems highly probable that John was familiar with Roman persecution and Christian martyrdom.

2. JOHN'S OTHER PURPOSES IN WRITING

These considerations concerning John's knowledge of Roman realities now having been presented, the way is open for an assessment of what John desired to indicate and emphasize in response to these realities. However, before embarking upon a systematic exposition of this study's thesis concerning John's purpose in this area, it will be helpful methodologically to note briefly several other purposes that have traditionally been ascribed to John. And second, it will also be useful to indicate expressly that the present study's range of concern does not encompass the other New Testament writings that have frequently been analyzed in conjunction with the Gospel.

At this juncture five of the purposes that have traditionally been attributed to John are appropriately considered. To begin with a purpose that is more general in scope, it has frequently been argued that John wrote principally to strengthen the faith of those who were already Christian, emphasizing to them that Jesus is truly the means of eternal life. Second, again generally, it has been argued that John's purpose was principally evangelistic, that is, he wrote to bring Jews and Gentiles alike to belief in Jesus as the Messiah and Son of God and the way to life everlasting.

The next kinds of purposes conjectured for John are more restricted in scope. One of these is that John intended his Gospel to serve as a bulwark against the persecutions of Jewish authorities who were hostile to the Christian movement just as the chief priests and Pharisees had been hostile to Jesus himself. A second circumscribed purpose is that John wrote to counter an unsaluatory influence by later disciples of John the Baptist who were advancing exaggerated claims on behalf of their mentor. Third, it is argued that John was conversant with Gnosticism and sought to counter certain aspects of this doctrine by indicating unequivocally that the Word of God had indeed become flesh in the person of Jesus.

How well does John's concern with Roman challenges, the purpose being argued for within this study, correspond with the five purposes just delineated? In the opening paragraphs of chapter one a certain compatibility and/or complementarity was suggested among several of the purposes more traditionally imputed to John and the "new" purpose attributed to him here. That fundamental compatibility is appropriately reemphasized now.

Without moving too far afield, it can be stated briefly that the general purpose of strengthening belief in Jesus is highly complementary to the thesis that John was concerned to respond to Roman challenges. For, as can readily be grasped, the theme of Jesus' sovereignty is of central importance to both of these purposes. Second, the theory that John's principal purpose was evangelism is not incompatible with a "Roman" purpose once it is accepted that John also intended to strengthen those converting for the challenges of Christian witness under Roman rule.

It is not within the purview of the present study to set forth a sustained brief in favor of one or other of the more general purposes. And much less is the objective to take up the arguments pro and con regarding each of the three more restricted purposes described above. Nevertheless, regardless of whether all of these latter three purposes or none of them are determined to be John's authentic intentions, little impact is made upon the argument presently being made for a Roman purpose. This point is to be emphasized specifically for the argument that John intended his Gospel as a bulwark against persecution from the Jewish authorities of his own day. This view may be placed side by side with the present interpretation regarding a Roman challenge to Christian belief. For conceivably, as discussed above in chapter six, John's readers might well have been persecuted both by synagogue officials and the Roman authorities. In both cases John's readers would be well served by the Gospel's emphasis upon Jesus' unsurpassed sovereignty.

Essentially, then, what is emphasized here is that John may well have had a variety of purposes in mind in setting forth his finished Gospel. Certainly among these purposes was the intention of guiding and supporting his readers in respect to the challenges they faced in their Roman surroundings.

Finally, this section is appropriately concluded by a paragraph locating the present study in reference to scholarly efforts to determine key features of the Christian community closest to John and in reference to scholarly attempts at determining the character of relationships and influences among John's Gospel, the Epistles of John, and the Revelation to John.

Such analyses are to be welcomed for the fresh insights that they succeed in bringing forward and the valuable contributions that they make to the study of the New Testament as a whole. However, it must be emphasized that the task of the present study has been to focus exclusively upon the Gospel of John as a work within its own integrity and standing. Indeed, one of the primary arguments of the present study is that the material present in the Gospel of John, in and of itself, is fully sufficient to warrant the conclusions that will now be elaborated.

3. TO PROVIDE SUPPORT FOR CHRISTIANS UNDER ROMAN RULE

The wording of the above heading is broadly phrased so as to allow for both a more restrictive thesis regarding Christians facing Roman persecution as well as a more general thesis concerning Christians challenged by Roman imperial claims. It will be the task of the following paragraphs to present the results of the previous analysis in terms of these two headings.

For both arguments, John's role in selecting material for inclusion within his final document and the precise way in which he ordered his presentation are of critical importance. Certainly other reports about Jesus could have been included, even other titles by which he was acclaimed. Certainly other reports about his disciples could also have been included. Nevertheless, these *are* the reports that John ultimately decided to present to his readers. What is more, he chose to use dramatic techniques to highlight the importance of at least three of the reports in question.

Surely the thoroughgoing emphasis upon the sovereignty of Jesus within John's Gospel is the first point to stress in any discussion of the present thesis regarding John's intention. However, except to note that Jesus is portrayed as a king within John's narrative (concerning which, see below), it is not necessary to review the numerous passages of the finished Gospel that attest to his sovereignty. Still it should be mentioned that these passages do constitute the general context for the specific reports which John includes concerning the sovereign titles by which Jesus is acclaimed.

As analyzed previously, there are three accolades for various Roman emperors that are predicated of Jesus within the Gospel of John. These titles are "Lord," "Savior of the world," and "Lord and God." "Lord" itself is quite extensively present, occurring unmodified or else with the modifiers, "the" or "my."

The net impact of these occurrences of "Lord," "the Lord," and "my Lord" is such as to illuminate that for those who believe in Jesus this title is one that expresses deep reverence and conviction. Caesar might be acclaimed as "lord" by many. But for those who recognize Jesus' true identity, *he* is the one who is ultimately Lord. John especially communicates this perspective by including a number of passages in which the title "Lord" is closely associated with Jesus' sovereignty over life and death.

In chapter four when the Samaritans' acclaim of Jesus as "Savior of the world" was first treated, it was observed that this title gathered up and culminated the meaning of other titles such as "prophet" and "messiah" that occurred earlier in Jesus' dialogue with the woman. It was also noted that several literary elements within the passage serve to establish that Jesus' role is savior of the *entire* world in a restrictive sense, i.e., that he *alone* accomplishes such a work. Let it now be reemphasized that it was John's intention to present this title in precisely such a manner.

Again, John was not compelled to include this particular passage within his finished account. Yet he *decided* to do so, and he presented Jesus' dialogue with the woman and the subsequent evangelizing efforts among the Samaritan townspeople in such a fashion that their confession of him as the Savior of the world emerges as the memorable apex of the entire episode.

Why did John so wish to emphasize that this title is one so fittingly used of Jesus? Why did he portray Jesus in other passages of his Gospel as the one who truly accomplishes the saving of the world? The contention of the present study is that John did so to encourage his readers not ever to be swayed or intimidated by the aggrandizing claims of the Roman emperors who styled themselves as saviors. Certainly other features present in this episode may have influenced John to include it in his final document. Yet surely he intended to stress that no other figure was comparable to Jesus for the saving of the world.

Similarly, with respect to the title "Lord and God," it is not merely that John attributes such a momentous title to Jesus in his finished account but also the fact that he does so in a context that heightens and enhances the meaning of these words. It has been observed that John positions Thomas' confession of Jesus as the culminating event of the first twenty chapters of the Gospel. So positioned, these words dramatically form an inclusion with the description of Jesus' exalted status given in the Gospel's prologue. What is more, the title's significance and richness also emerge because it blends the objective and subjective dimensions of Jesus' lordship that have already been presented in John 20.

As previously noted, prior to Thomas' confession, Jesus has already been referred to by Mary Magdalene and the other disciples as "the Lord," and Mary Magdalene has also poignantly referred to him as "my Lord." Thomas' magnificent acclamation thus blends both of these dimensions and combines them remarkably with the "lord and god" phrase so prominent and controversial in Roman circles.

Surely it was John's intention that, when his readers began to grasp these rich meanings, they would thereby find themselves instructed and encouraged. For John, Jesus is so essentially Lord and God that it is blasphemous for such titles to be applied to any other figure. And John is an author who is wonderfully sensitive to the way in which an episode can be described in such a literary fashion as to engage one's readers to the maximum degree.

Is John not thus seeking to stress to his readers with the final scene of chapter 20 that Jesus must be their Lord and God in as deeply a personal way as he finally was for Thomas? Is John not encouraging his readers to reject the idolatrous pretensions of any other figure who might seek the mantle of such a title? Ultimately for John there is only one who is truly Lord and God just as there is only one who is *truly* the Savior of the world.

And this is the fundamental truth that he intended to impart to his readers using his finest literary gifts.

There may well not be a better starting point for establishing the relevance of this Gospel for the situation of Christians facing Roman threats than the Roman trial of Jesus detailed within John 18 and 19. Jesus' kingship, as that narrative discloses, does not involve any attempt to supplant Roman rule by violent means. As indicated in chapter five above, advertance to this fact could well have constituted a valuable point of defense for Christians being interrogated by Roman authorities. However, perhaps even more relevant for a situation in which Christians were already guilty by reason of their name, was Jesus' example in bearing witness to the truth. Jesus inviting Pilate to belief may well have been another aspect of Jesus' trial conduct that John wanted his readers to be familiar with.

The present study's more restricted argument concerning John's response to Roman persecution is now appropriately made. Like the argument regarding John's purpose of counteracting the imperial cult, this argument also relies fundamentally upon (a) the presence of abundant material within John's text pertaining to persecution and faithful perseverance, and (b) John's artful ordering of much of this material in order to achieve a maximum impact upon his readers.

Chapter six above explored the effect that Jesus' farewell discourses could well have had upon readers besieged in various ways by Roman persecution. It now suffices to list the subject headings under which Jesus' words were then analyzed. It should be recalled here that John necessarily made careful decisions regarding how much material to include on a particular topic when he fashioned his Gospel. Certainly he may well have had other purposes for presenting Jesus' farewell discourses as they now appear, yet clearly he has included a goodly amount of material pertaining to the withstanding of persecution.

First, John portrays Jesus predicting that his disciples would experience persecution in the time ahead. Second, Jesus warns of the danger of apostasy as a consequence of such persecution. Third, in memorable words and images he stresses the importance of their remaining closely bonded with him. And fourth, he stresses the importance of their love for one another. Jesus' final words in virtually each one of these categories would have been highly relevant to Christians in circumstances corresponding with those that have been established for the Christians of Bithynia-Pontus under Pliny.

In addition, Jesus also provided his disciples with other forms of assurance in these discourses. He consoled them with the word that he was departing to prepare a place for them with the Father. He alerted them to the continued presence of the evil one but indicated his own power for surpassing Satan; he prayed that they would be preserved from the evil one's influence. Further, the Holy Spirit would be their Paraclete, assisting them to confess their belief and to act forthrightly against the ruler of this world. Finally, Jesus assured them that the ultimate outcome would be their victory. For he himself had overcome the world, and the Father had given him the power to bring all those entrusted to him to eternal life.

These then would be extraordinarily rich themes for Christians under persecution to ponder and pray over. And John also included within his final account two sets of contrasting images that can be readily appreciated in terms of the potential for encouraging beleaguered Christians. Meditation upon the contrasting proclamations "Jesus of Nazareth the king of the Jews" and "We have no king but Caesar" would be strength-engendering. Meditation upon the two contrasting images involving friendship would be still more so. In circumstances in which what is at issue is the laying down of one's life for one's friend, how poignant is the concept of friendship with Jesus! Clearly it would be more preferable to lose one's life in this world for the sake of friendship with Jesus than to be compromised into striving for "friendship" with Caesar.

The theme of gaining one's life through Jesus is also highlighted in the personal note that John includes for his readers at the end of chapter 20. It was established by Trajan's rescript that perseverance in bearing the name of Christian would entail the loss of one's life. How striking then that in his own solemn author's note John emphasizes that it is precisely in Jesus' name that they have life! Again, other factors may have made such a reference an attractive one for John. Nevertheless, to include such an encouraging statement at just such a juncture comports well with the argument that John really was consciously trying to strengthen those of his readers who faced a severe testing "for the name."

Finally, the present argument regarding John's response to a situation of persecution also receives support from the careful manner in which John presents and then elaborates upon the matter of Peter's own martyrdom. It has been previously affirmed that the mere allusion to Roman crucifixion as Peter's fate provides a sound basis for the judgment that John had knowledge about Roman hostility. Now what is being proposed is that John's nuanced juxtaposition of Peter's life course with the "remaining" of the beloved disciple indicates the evangelist's intention to leave his readers with two instructive and memorable images related to martyrdom and community life.

In effect, by reason of his careful presentation here, John intended that his readers ponder fully Jesus' imperative that some of his disciples, including some with pastoral office, were called to follow him into Roman crucifixion. Others, however, were called to abide, to *remain* with Jesus, expressing their faithfulness in other forms—even to the writing of a Gospel. Once again, what a summoning conclusion for John to impart to Christian communities in which each form of witness was then being lived out.

Given the presence of such a scene imaging martyrdom and *remaining* at the end of his account and given the presence with the body of the Gospel of all of the above considered passages pertaining to persecution, the present study contends that John did indeed write to provide encouragement for Christians who were proximate to such an experience in their lives with the Roman empire. John himself lived within the Roman empire and knew its premises and its operations fully well. He especially recognized the threat posed to Christian faith by the cult of the emperors, and he consciously sought to counteract these exaggerated, idolatrous claims with the material about Jesus that he included in his final text.

When both of these aspects of the evangelist's work are adequately considered, his Gospel does indeed emerge in a new perspective. John undoubtedly had a variety of reasons for publishing the Gospel in exactly its present form. Yet certainly among these reasons was his intention to present elements and themes that were significant for Christians facing Roman imperial claims and for any who faced Roman persecution.

Appendix 1

Pliny's Letter to Trajan X.96

It is my custom to refer all my difficulties to you, Sir, for no one is better able to resolve my doubts and to inform my ignorance.

I have never been present at an examination of Christians. Consequently, I do not know the nature or the extent of the punishments usually meted out to them, nor the grounds for starting an investigation and how far it should be pressed. Nor am I at all sure whether any distinction should be made between them on the grounds of age, or if young people and adults should be treated alike; whether a pardon ought to be granted to anyone retracting his beliefs, or if he has once professed Christianity, he shall gain nothing by renouncing it; and whether it is the mere name of Christian which is punishable, even if innocent of crime, or rather the crimes associated with the name.

For the moment this is the line I have taken with all persons brought before me on the charge of being Christians. I have asked them in person if they are Christians, and if they admit it, I repeat the question a second and third time, with a warning of the punishment awaiting them. If they persist, I order them to be led away for execution; for whatever the nature of their admission, I am convinced that their stubbornness and unshakeable obstinacy ought not to go unpunished. There have been others similarly fanatical who are Roman citizens. I have entered them on the list of persons to be sent to Rome for trial.

Now that I have begun to deal with this problem, as so often happens, the charges are becoming more widespread and increasing in variety. An anonymous pamphlet has been circulated which contains the names of a number of accused persons. Among these I considered that I should dismiss any who denied that they were or ever had been Christians when they had repeated after me a formula of invocation to the gods and had made offerings of wine and incense to your statue (which I had ordered to be brought into court for this purpose along with the images of the gods), and furthermore had reviled the name of Christ: none of which things, I understand, any genuine Christian can be induced to do.

Others, whose names were given to me by an informer, first admitted the charge and then denied it; they said that they had ceased to be Christians two or more years previously, and some of them even twenty years ago. They all did reverence to your statue and the images of the gods in the same way as the others, and reviled the name of Christ. They also declared that the sum total of their guilt or error amounted to no more than this: they had met regularly before dawn on a fixed day to chant verses alternately among themselves in honour of Christ as if to a god, and also to bind themselves by oath, not for any criminal purpose, but to abstain from theft, robbery and adultery, to commit no breach of trust and not to deny a deposit when called upon to restore it. After this ceremony it had been their custom to disperse and reassemble later to take food of an ordinary, harmless kind; but they had in fact given up this practice since my edict, issued on your instructions, which banned all political societies. This made me decide it was all the more necessary to extract the truth by torture from two slave-women, whom they called deaconesses. I found nothing but a degenerate sort of cult carried to extravagant lengths.

I have therefore postponed any further examination and hastened to consult you. The question seems to me to be worthy of your consideration, especially in view of the number of persons endangered; for a great many individuals of every age and class, both men and women, are being brought to trial, and this is likely to continue. It is not only the towns, but villages and rural districts too which are infected through contact with this wretched cult. I think though that it is still possible for it to be checked and directed to better ends, for there is no doubt that people have begun to throng the temples which had been almost entirely deserted for a long time; the sacred rites which had been allowed to lapse are being performed again, and flesh of sacrificial victims is on sale everywhere, though up till recently scarcely anyone could be found to buy it. It is easy to infer from this that a great many people could be reformed if they were given an opportunity to repent.

Appendix 2

Trajan's Rescript X.97

You have followed the right course of procedure, my dear Pliny, in your examination of the cases of persons charged with being Christians, for it is impossible to lay down a general rule to a fixed formula. These people must not be hunted out; if they are brought before you and the charge against them is proved, they must be punished, but in the case of anyone who denies that he is a Christian, and makes it clear that he is not by offering prayers to our gods, he is to be pardoned as a result of his repentance however suspect his past conduct may be. But pamphlets circulated anonymously must play no part in any accusation. They create the worst sort of precedent and are quite out of keeping with the spirit of our age.

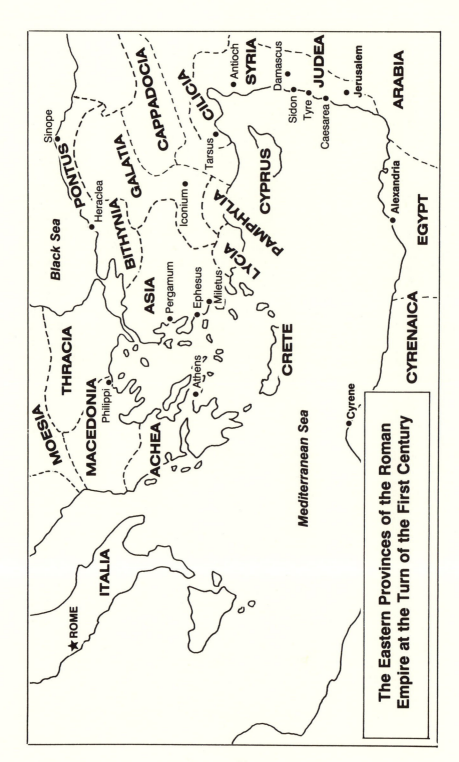

The Eastern Provinces of the Roman Empire at the Turn of the First Century

92

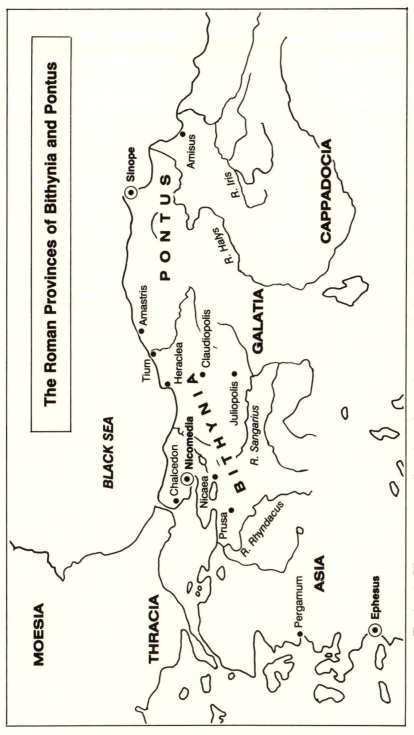

The Roman Provinces of Bithynia and Pontus

The legate Pliny was proceeding along the northern coastal rim of Bithynia-Pontus at the time of his correspondence with Trajan regarding his procedures against the Christians of this province.

Notes

Chapter One: Orientation to John's Gospel

1. The well regarded commentaries in the select bibliography for this study are representative of the traditional and contemporary approaches to John's Gospel. One searches in vain within these works for any explicit reference to the idea that John was responding to Roman factors when he published his Gospel.

2. R. Kysar, *The Fourth Evangelist and His Gospel* (Minneapolis: Augsburg, 1975), pp. 147-165 and R. Culpepper, *Anatomy of the Fourth Gospel* (Minneapolis: Fortress, 1983), p. 21, provide helpful overviews of representative scholars who have argued on behalf of one or more of these purposes. See chapter eight below for a more extended presentation as to how such purposes are congruent with the purpose being argued for in this study.

3. Representative of the commentators who ably defend a complex view of authorship is R. Brown, *The Gospel According to John* (Garden City: Doubleday, 1966-71; hereafter "Brown"), vol. 1, pp. lxxxvii-cii, and *The Gospel and Epistles of John: A Concise Commentary* (Collegeville: Liturgical Press, 1988), pp. 11-12. A recent commentary defending the more traditional view of authorship is D. A. Carson, *The Gospel According to John* (Grand Rapids: Eerdmans, 1991; hereafter "Carson"), pp. 68-81.

4. B. Lindars is a leading exponent of the theory that preached homilies served as sources for a substantial portion of the Gospel. See his *Behind the Fourth Gospel* (London: SPCK, 1971), pp. 46-47 and *The Gospel of John* (Grand Rapids: Eerdmans, 1972; hereafter "Lindars"), pp. 51-53.

5. E. Haenchen, *A Commentary on the Gospel of John* (Minneapolis: Fortress, 1984; hereafter "Haenchen"), vol. 1, pp. 45-51, provides a helpful discussion of the procedures that seemingly governed the physical production of the text of the Gospel. In his view, the Gospel was probably copied onto a codex rather than a scroll (p. 48).

6. As an indication of one eminent scholar's approach to the question of the Gospel's date, the work of Brown, vol. 1, p. lxxxvi, may be cited. Brown argues for 75-110 as the outer boundaries for the publication of the Gospel with the decade of the 90s as probable and a year close to 100 as plausible. However, it must be noted that this is the date for *the final edition* of the Gospel; in Brown's view a first edition of the work may well have been achieved earlier, possibly between 70 and 85.

7. Haenchen, pp. 6-18, identifies and discusses the comments of thirteen early Christian writers and documents relative to the Gospel of John. See also Carson, pp. 23-29.

8. In order to provide a sense of the complexity (and uncertainty) regarding

the place of John's Gospel, the positions taken by B. Lindars and R. Schnackenburg in their respective commentaries can be cited. While favoring Ephesus slightly, Lindars, pp. 43-44, expresses support for Syria while minimizing the possibility of either Alexandria or Palestine. Approaching the question from the standpoint of the religious factors that presumably influenced the Gospel, Schnackenburg, *The Gospel According to St. John* (New York: Crossroad, 1990; hereafter "Schnackenburg"), vol. 1, pp. 149-152, sees no fundamental objection to Ephesus but also notes various factors in favor of Egypt (less likely), Palestine, or Syria. However, Schnackenburg's final hypothesis is predicated upon a fluid Johannine tradition that originated in Palestine and developed in Syria before being finally fixed and edited in Ephesus.

9. As discussed above, the final text of the Gospel was eventually made available in scroll and/or in codex form. Very likely it was "circulated" among members of only one community (Was the first use primarily liturgical?) before copies were made for wider distribution. However, it may not be ruled out that several scrolls and/or codices were produced from the original before any public circulation occurred. And thus it is not inconceivable that the final version of the Fourth Gospel was initially available in several communities as opposed to just one. Certainly over an interval of time the circulation of the final text extended to Christian communities in every part of the empire.

Chapter Two: The Jewish Tax and the Cult of Rome's Emperors

1. The primary Roman sources for developments related to the Flavian dynasty are Suetonius, *The Lives of the Caesars* (Cambridge, Massachusetts: Loeb Classical Library, 1939) 8; Dio Cassius, *Dio's Roman History* (New York: Loeb Classical Library, 1939) 65-67; Tacitus, *The Histories* (New York: Loeb Classical Library, 1925-31). For a clear assessment, see M. Charlesworth, "The Flavian Dynasty," *Cambridge Ancient History*, vol. 11 (New York: Macmillan, 1936), pp. 1-44.

2. H.S.J. Hart describes and analyzes the various coins minted and circulated throughout the empire to underscore the significance of this Flavan victory. See H.S.J. Hart, "Judea and Rome: The Official Commentary," *Journal of Theological Studies*, N.S. vol. 3, pt. 2 (1952), pp. 172-204, Hart indicates just how thoroughly this endeavor was undertaken: "The emphasis is great indeed. It is in all metals — not only gold and silver, it is on the poor man's brass, the money of the people, even to the little quadrans with its emblematic palm-tree ... It comes from all mints — from Spain, Rome, Gaul, Syria, and elsewhere. . . . The whole empire must concentrate on the one theme — *IUDEA CAPTA* (p. 184).

3. For an analysis of this practice and the argument that this didrachma was paid to the Jerusalem temple as a *contribution* rather than as a *tax*, see R. Cassidy, "Matthew 17:24-27 — A Word on Civil Taxes," *Catholic Biblical Quarterly* 41 (1979), pp. 571-574. Obviously once victorious Rome redirected this payment to the Capitoline temple, there was no longer a voluntary dimension to it; it was then, in effect, an especially odious *tax*.

4. According to Philo, *The Embassy to Gaius* (New York: Loeb Classical Library, 1930, 1942) 40, and Josephus, *Jewish Antiquities* (New York: Loeb Classical Library, 1930) XVI.6.2-7, Augustus and Tiberius were both accommodating in this regard.

5. In *The Jewish War* (New York: Loeb Classical Library, 1928) 7.6.6., Josephus

describes Vespasian's enactment of the tax as follows: "On all Jews, wheresoever resident, he imposed a poll-tax of two drachmas to be paid annually into the Capitol as formerly contributed by them to the temple at Jerusalem." Cf. Dio Cassius, *Dio's Roman History* 66.7. For surviving records documenting the payment of this tax by Jews resident in the province of Egypt from the time of Vespasian forward, see V. Tcherikover and A. Kuks, eds., *Corpus Papyrorum Judicarum*, vol. 2 (Cambridge, Massachusetts: Harvard University Press, 1960), pp. 119-136.

6. This view is expressed by J. Rolfe, the translator for Suetonius, *The Lives of the Caesars*, in an explanatory note, p. 366. So also P. Keresztes, "The Jews, the Christians, and the Emperor Domitian," *Vigiliae Christianae* 27 (1973), p. 5.

7. This translation is given by H. Mattingly, *Coins of the Roman Empire in the British Museum*, vol. 3 (London: The Trustees of the British Museum, 1966), p. xlviii. I am indebted to Fr. Thomas Bermingham, SJ, from the Fordham University Classics Department and to Professor David Daube from the Law Faculty of the University of California at Berkeley for assistance in investigating this inscription.

8. Ibid.

9. Tcherikover and Kuks, *Corpus Papyrorum Judiacarum*, pp. 119-136.

10. The view of the imperial cult presented in this section generally reflects the presentations made by M. Charlesworth, "Some Observations on Ruler-Cult Especially in Rome," *Harvard Theological Review* 28 (1935), pp. 5-44, and more recently, S. Price, *Rituals and Power: The Roman Imperial Cult in Asia Minor* (Cambridge: Cambridge University Press, 1984). Charlesworth and Price both advert to the distinct dimensions of the Greek and Latin approaches to the cult and both, while differing in degree, recognize the difficulty in determining the precise standing accorded to a particular emperor within the developing cult. For additional perspective on the era of Vespasian and Domitian, see W. Frend, *Martyrdom and Persecution in the Early Church* (Grand Rapids: Baker, 1981), pp. 193-194.

11. M. Charlesworth, "Some Observations on Ruler-Cult Especially in Rome," pp. 32-35.

12. This usage is documented by D. Magie, *De romanorum iuris publici sacrique vocabulis sollemnibus in graecum sermonem conversis* (Leipzig: Teubner, 1905), pp. 67-68, and cited by A. Deissmann, *Light from the Ancient East* (Grand Rapids: Baker, 1965), p. 364. It is also cited and presented by C. Koester, "The Savior of the World (John 4:42)," *Journal of Biblical Literature* 109 (1990), p. 667.

13. A. Deissmann, *Light from the Ancient East*, pp. 364-365, relying on work by F. Blumenthal and W. Dittenberger.

14. Ibid. p. 353. W. Boussuet, *Kyrios Christos* (Nashville: Abingdon, 1970), pp. 138-140, describes the prior usage of comparable terms for various rulers within Egypt.

15. A. Deissmann, *Light from the Ancient East*, p. 353.

16. Ibid. pp. 353-354. Here Deissmann discusses the use of "lord" for Nero in Egypt, in Greece, and in Italy by a king from Persia arriving to do homage to the emperor. Regarding its use in Egypt Deissmann writes: "At any rate the statistics are quite striking; everywhere down to the remotest village, the officials called Nero *Kyrios*." Regarding its use in Greece he writes: "It is a very important fact that under Nero we first find the *Kyrios*-title in an inscription in Greece. The marble tablet of Acraephiae in Boeotia ... which immortalizes, among other things, a speech made by Nero at Corinth in November 67, contains a decree of honor in which the Boeotian town calls him once 'lord of the whole world,' and then, what

is in my opinion more important simply 'the lord Augustus,' divine honors being awarded him by the decree." Regarding usage in an Italian setting Deissmann writes: "Tiridates came from the East to Italy and did homage to Nero at Naples as 'the lord' and in Rome as 'the god.' "

17. Ibid., p. 355.

18. M. Charlesworth, "Some Observations on Ruler-Cult Especially in Rome," p. 35, emphasizes Pliny's use of this term in reference to Trajan and also refers to inscriptions that appear to confer *dominus* or *dominus noster* officially upon Hadrian.

19. It must again be observed that only miniscule data for the use of these titles has survived. Thus it is at least conceivable that "lord and god" or some comparable honorific had been bestowed upon a previous emperor or emperors before Domitian arrogated it to himself. In this connection the reference to Augustus in Egypt as "the god and lord Emperor" (see note 14 above), and Tiridates' references to Nero as "the lord" at Naples and as "the god" at Rome (see note 16 above) should be recalled.

Chapter Three: Pliny, Trajan, and the Christians of Pontus

1. In the section of his comprehensive volume that discusses the nature of Pliny's assignment to Bithynia-Pontus, A. N. Sherwin-White, *The Letters of Pliny* (Oxford: Clarendon, 1966) emphasizes that Pliny received *imperium* from Trajan but along with it a set of *mandata* that limited the exercise of *imperium*. As a consequence of these *mandata*, Pliny would be encouraged to be regularly in contact with Trajan (p. 547).

2. This idea is expressed at 35,4 of *Panegyricus*, the extended work of praise that Pliny addressed to Trajan out of gratitude for his appointment as consul. See Pliny, *Letters and Panegyricus* (Cambridge, Massachusetts: Loeb Classical Library, 1969; hereafter *Letters*). B. Radice's introduction to her translation of these works, pp. ix-xxvi, is deserving of mention in its own right.

3. Pliny expresses this sentiment in his letter to Caninius Rufus (*Letters* VIII. 4,5). Perspective on Pliny's attitude toward the ruler cult in general and Trajan in particular is given in K. Scott, "The Elder and Younger Pliny on Emperor Worship," *Transactions of the American Philological Association* 63 (1932), pp. 156-165. For the interpretation that Pliny's excessive enthusiasm can be explained, in part, by his belief that Domitian's excesses were finally over, see M. Charlesworth, "Some Observations on Ruler-Cult Especially in Rome" (see chapter 2, n. 10 above), p. 38.

4. R. Wilken, *The Christians as the Romans Saw Them* (New Haven: Yale University Press, 1984), pp. 10-15, provides a concise overview of the context in Bithynia-Pontus and the principal matters with which Pliny was to deal.

5. Sherwin-White, *The Letters of Pliny*, p. 80, considers it possible that Pliny may have gone to Bithynia-Pontus as early as 109. He places this particular letter between 18 September and 3 January of Pliny's second year (p. 691).

6. Pliny, *Letters* X.96,7-8.

7. Pliny, *Letters* X.96,10.

8. In his shorter work, *Fifty Letters of Pliny* (Oxford: Oxford University Press, 1967), p. 174, Sherwin-White comments upon the implications of the phrase *nomen*

ipsum as it occurs in Pliny's letter X.96,2. He alludes to the view of Tertullian that such a charge was especially destructive because it gave Christians no opportunity to display the innocence of their lives. While Tertullian attributes the invention of this procedure to Nero, Sherwin-White notes that the Romans had even earlier used such forms of prosecution against other sects, e.g., worshipers of Bacchus.

9. Given the particular character of the present study, it is not necessary to enter into the controversies surrounding two of the major issues related to the persecution of Christians. For, on the one hand, the Roman measures against Christians need not be continuous or empire-wide in order for them to have elicited a response from John. Nor do the "legal" grounds on which the Romans proceeded have to be established precisely. It suffices that at least some Christians were executed because they were Christians during the reign of Nero and that at least some trials involving Christians were held at the end of Domitian's reign and/or at the beginning of Trajan's.

Sherwin-White's overview in his appendix to *The Letters of Pliny*, pp. 772-787, including the issues he alludes to in his discussion with G. de Ste-Croix, provides a useful *status questionis* relative to the two issues just mentioned. Sherwin-White's own view on the extent of the persecutions is concisely stated in his *Fifty Letters of Pliny*, p. 173: "So in circumstances that are not clear, the Christians from A.D. 65 onward came to be regarded as practitioners of an undesirable cult and could be prosecuted as such, following a precedent established by Nero. . . . The enforcement of such bans depended in Roman legal usage upon the activity of unofficial accusers of *delatores*. . . . There was no public prosecutor for this or any crime in the Roman world. Hence the 'persecution' of Christians was very limited and occasional during the first two centuries A.D., even when governors accepted the evidence of mere informers."

10. Considerable meaning resides in Pliny's use of the technical term *cognitio* here. What is indicated is that Christians had already been subject to officially authorized, public trials (in contrast with lesser proceedings or spontaneous actions by adversaries of Christians) years before members of the Christian community in Bithynia-Pontus ever appeared at Pliny's tribunal. Sherwin-White, *The Letters of Pliny*, p. 694, deduces that these earlier trials were held at Rome. Sherwin-White then provides the following explanation of what was involved in a *cognitio* and how Pliny would have been familiar with the general character of such trials even though he had not been present for those involving Christians: "The term *cognitio* confirms . . . that the form of trial was the personal judgment of the holder of *imperium* sitting formally *pro tribunali* to hear charges made in due form, and assisted by his *consilium*. He may be the proconsul or the imperial legate in provinces, or the city prefect who excercised the main police supervision at Rome with capital powers . . . Pliny had some experience of *cognitio* procedure when prefect of Saturn . . . and as assessor in Trajan's personal court" (p. 695).

11. In "The Jews, the Christians and Emperor Domitian," *Vigilae Christianae* 27 (1973), p. 22, P. Keresztes expresses the view that Pliny may have actually known more about these trials than he indicates in his letter to Trajan. Keresztes bases his view on the fact that Pliny has unhesitatingly employed extremely effective procedures for separating committed Christians from the others denounced to him, i.e., the offering of wine and incense to the gods and the emperor's image and cursing the name of Christ. How did Pliny arrive at such "effective" tests? Pliny himself seems to imply that an informer provided him such information. However,

Keresztes argues that these techniques had actually emerged at the earlier trials, which in Keresztes' estimation were part of a more general persecution under Domitian.

12. R. Wilken, *The Christians as the Romans Saw Them*, p. 22, observes that Pliny's behavior here is at variance with his customary deliberateness. In effect, Pliny has already used capital punishment for a number of Christians before ascertaining from Trajan whether such executions are really "required." Presumably Pliny must have had some reason causing him to think that his actions were appropriate. Wilken also suggests that Pliny may have known more about the earlier trials of Christians than he indicates in his letter. This in turn raises the issue of whether there was already some "custom" for executing Christians because they were Christians. If some form of precedent existed, then Trajan's rescript confirmed rather than established such measures.

13. Sherwin-White, *The Letters of Pliny*, p. 698, indicates the following in his note on Pliny's word *duci*: "They are led off to immediate execution by the sword, like the men of Scilli. This use of *duci* is common enough. . . . Pliny did not reserve them for a death in the amphitheatre, like that of Ignatius under Trajan, or Polycarp and the Lyons martyrs later in the century."

14. Pliny, *Letters* X.96,4.

15. Wilken, *The Christians as the Romans Saw Them*, pp. 25-27, sketches the prior history of the Roman custom of offering wine and incense in supplication and emphasizes that Pliny has incorporated this practice into a test of allegiance. Without adverting to the significant fact that this test now involves obeisance to the statue of the emperor (Trajan), Wilken does refer to the possibility that Pliny may have derived the idea for the test from some of Domitian's practices.

16. Significantly, *The Martyrdom of St. Polycarp* (Westminster, Maryland: Newman, 1948) indicates (8.2; 9.3) that these same two tests were at issue when Polycarp was faced with the loss of his life at Smyrna of the adjacent province of Asia approximately forty-five years later in the year 150. The following memorable dialogue is recorded in 8.2 as two Roman officials try to persuade Polycarp to capitulate. Note the subsequent significance of attributing the title "lord" to a Roman emperor is also indicated here: "Really," they said, "what harm is there in saying 'Lord Caesar' and offering incense—and what goes with it—and being saved?" At first he did not answer them; but when they persisted, he said: "I am not going to do what you counsel me."

17. Pliny, *Letters* X.96,5.

18. Sherwin-White, *The Letters of Pliny*, p. 709, argues that a problem in the text should be resolved by reading *carnem*. And thus Pliny's sense is that the number of those who refrain from purchasing the sacrificial meat has been greatly diminished as a consequence of his own pressures against the Christians.

19. Wilken, *The Christians as the Romans Saw Them*, provides a useful overview regarding *hetaeria* and *superstitio*, the two terms Pliny uses in characterizing Christians. On p. 34 he indicates that *hetaeria* can be translated "political club" or "association," but its meaning is broad enough to enable Pliny to use it in referring to a firefighter's club in Nicomedia in another of his letters. On pp. 48-50 Wilken directs attention to the fact that Tacitus and Suetonius, contemporaries of Pliny, both used *superstitio* ("superstition") in their own brief references to the Christian movement.

20. Again the fact that Pliny seemingly presumed the existence of Christians'

capital liability when he wrote to Trajan should not be lost sight of. Pliny had already executed some Christians on this basis, but subsequently had second thoughts about whether he should continue to do so. What Trajan's reply thus signals is that there will be no turning back from this approach of executing persevering Christians.

21. The unelaborated, even terse, character of Trajan's reply on this primary matter deserves emphasis. Sherwin-White, *The Letters of Pliny*, p. 696, comments upon this feature of the rescript with the perhaps undue understatement: "Trajan's too brief reply confirms this procedure without explaining the grounds for it."

22. Sherwin-White, *The Letters of Pliny*, p. 712, emphasizes that Trajan's according of pardon to those who indicated repentance through Pliny's tests allows a procedure that is otherwise unknown within Roman criminal law. As a possible explanation for such a measure, Sherwin-White conjectures that Trajan and his advisors may have entered upon a strategy of seeking to undermine the Christian movement from within.

23. Sherwin-White, *The Letters of Pliny*, pp. 711, 782.

24. Sherwin-White, *The Letters of Pliny*, believes that the rescript had limited consequences within the empire as a whole. The governors of other provinces may have followed it as an *exemplum*, but it was not a law for the whole empire (p. 711). Concerning the idea that a collection of official documents pertaining to Christians might have been circulated, such a step seemingly did not occur before Ulpian (p. 783). Even within Bithynia-Pontus the rescript would not have been automatically binding upon Pliny's successors unless Trajan specifically included it within the *mandata* he issued to them (p. 783). Sherwin-White's overall view is thus that, despite the rescript, official Roman measures against Christians continued to be highly sporadic until the Decian persecutions began (p. 783; see the presentation of his views given in note 9 above).

Chapter Four: The Sovereignty of Jesus

1. For a concise analysis of the way in which John's Gospel emphasizes christology, see Schnackenburg, vol. 1, pp. 154-156. Also see the author's third excursus, pp. 507-514, for a discussion of the remarkable array of titles that delineate Jesus' identity in John's first chapter. Jesus' identity in John is analyzed in terms of "incarnational christology" by R. Kysar, *John, The Maverick Gospel* (Atlanta: Knox, 1976), pp. 29-31. That John succeeds in presenting the exalted Jesus in such a way that he *really* lives in the world is well reflected upon by D. M. Smith, "The Presentation of Jesus in the Fourth Gospel," *Interpretation* 31 (1977), pp. 376-377.

2. Schnackenburg, vol. 1, pp. 230-231, finds the origins of John's prologue in a Christian logos-hymn. The apex of the first verse comes in the statement that the Word was God (p. 234). Verse 14's statement that the Word became flesh hearkens back to verse 1 and represents the climax of the prologue as a whole (p. 266).

3. While there are difficulties with the text of this verse, the leading variations all attest to the unsurpassed revealing power of Jesus. Because of his intimacy with the Father, no one else reveals as does the Son. Brown, vol. 1, pp. 17-18, provides a lucid discussion of the principal possibilities regarding the preferred text. As Brown additionally points out, p. 36, several elements in the verse adroitly form inclusions with key elements in 1:1. Thus, for example, in both verse 18 and verse 1, the Word/the Son is immediately present with God.

4. See S. Smalley, *John: Evangelist and Interpreter* (Exeter: Pater Noster, 1978), pp. 86-92, for the argument that Jesus' signs and discourses, along with the "I am" sayings, have been arranged in such a way as to contribute to the overall unity of John's Gospel.

5. See R. Fortna, "Theological Use of Locale in the Fourth Gospel," *Anglican Theological Review* s.s. 3 (1974), pp. 58-95, for a thorough treatment of Jesus' geographical movements in John's Gospel.

6. For a comprehensive treatment of the various dimensions of belief in John's account see Schnackenburg's fine excursus "The Notion of Faith in the Fourth Gospel," vol. 1, pp. 558-575. P. Minear, "The Audience of the Fourth Evangelist," *Interpretation* 31 (1977), pp. 351-352, suggests that the multiple gradations and forms of faith present in the Gospel reflect the arduousness of truly believing in the name of Jesus.

7. The importance of Jesus' self-designation as "the Son" for John's overall christology is emphasized and analyzed by Schnackenburg, vol. 2, pp. 172-177.

8. Brown's appendix, *"Egō eimi—I am,"* vol. 1, pp. 533-538, provides a comprehensive treatment of the three types of usage within John's Gospel and indicates the extraordinary claim that is involved when Jesus speaks these words absolutely.

9. Drawing upon Brown's analysis, R. Kysar, *John, The Maverick Gospel,* pp. 43-44, holds that when Jesus pronounces "I am" absolutely, he is actually pronouncing the sacred name of God (thereby indicating that he *is* God). Brown, vol. 1, p. 537, points out that the response of Jesus' hearers at 8:58 and 18:5 testifies to the implications of divinity that are present in these words. In the former case, Jesus' hearers attempt to stone him; in the latter, the arresting party falls to the ground.

10. Contra Smalley, *John: Evangelist and Interpreter*, pp. 86-88, who holds for John 21:1-14 (the miraculous catch of 153 fish) as a seventh sign, it seems preferable to follow C. H. Dodd, *The Interpretation of the Fourth Gospel* (Cambridge: Cambridge University Press, 1953), pp. 289ff, and Brown, vol. 1, pp. cxxxviii-cxxix, in regarding Jesus' walking upon the Sea of Galilee as a fifth sign, with the result that the raising of Lazarus is a culminating seventh sign. Instead of counting the miraculous catch of fish as an additional discrete sign, is this episode not more appropriately regarded as helping to form the continuous stream of miraculous conduct that is the hallmark of the risen Jesus in John 20 and John 21?

11. A suggestive treatment of the linkage between believing in Jesus' word and attaining eternal life is given in P. Minear, *John: The Martyr's Gospel* (New York: Pilgrim Press, 1984), pp. 92-102.

12. See 1:48 and 4:16-19 for other instances of Jesus' supra-human knowledge.

13. Jesus' concluding comment at the end of his dialogue again expresses his knowledge of betrayal by one of them who "is a devil," and John adds a narrator's comment that Jesus was referring to Judas (6:70-71).

14. The concept of Jesus' "hour" is an extremely substantial theme within John's Gospel. See, for example, Brown, vol. 1, pp. 517-518, and I. de la Potterie, *The Hour of Jesus* (New York: Alba House, 1989). It is only at 12:23, after Jesus has raised Lazarus and has returned to Jerusalem for the final time, that he proclaims that his hour has arrived. This hour is not an hour of darkness, but rather is the hour of his elevation on the cross and his exaltation.

15. A. Harvey, *Jesus on Trial* (London: SCM, 1976) repeatedly points to the

strategic steps and evasive maneuvers that John presents Jesus utilizing during the course of his public ministry.

16. Within the limits of this study the various means by which John's reports indicate the tensions present in the interval prior to Jesus' final entry into Jerusalem cannot be alluded to. One does sense that Jesus is safe as long as he chooses to remain outside of Judea proper (see 11:54). Nevertheless, he sovereignly chooses to return to Bethany for a gathering with Lazarus, Martha, and Mary, and thence to a dramatic entrance into Jerusalem itself. See R. Fortna, "The Theological Use of Locale in the Fourth Gospel," pp. 79-81, for more detailed comments regarding Jesus' movements here.

17. Beyond the ways mentioned in the text, John's patterns of depicting Jesus as the fulfillment of Scripture and as "replacing" the leading institutions, customs, and feasts of Judaism should also be noted. See, for example, the specific comments of Carson, pp. 263, 287, 391, and 399, and the general statements by G. Yee, *Jewish Feasts and the Gospel of John* (Collegeville: Liturgical Press, 1989), pp. 60, 82.

18. As will be seen in chapters six and seven, the word *menō* is rich in theological content within John's Gospel; the disciples *remaining* bonded with Jesus is of the utmost importance. Something of this meaning may well be contained in the present verse. C. K. Barrett, *The Gospel According to St. John* (Philadelphia: Westminster, 1978; hereafter "Barrett"), p. 243, perceptively comments that this *temporary* dwelling with the Samaritans, limited to two days, looks ahead to the *remaining* without end that will be possible after Jesus' glorification and the coming of the Spirit.

19. On the relationship between these titles, M-J. Lagrange, *Évangile selon Saint Jean* (Paris: Gabalda, 1936; hereafter "Lagrange"), p. 122, comments that the Samaritan use of "Savior of the world" enables them to acclaim Jesus by a title that is more comprehensive than "messiah." Barrett, p. 244, comments that, within this episode, John is very definitely concerned to present Jesus as the messiah of Judaism; however, John insists that this term (and all others) be understood in the widest sense.

20. C. Koester, "The Savior of the World (John 4:42)," p. 668, rightly emphasizes that this title transcends the traditional meanings associated with Samaritan or Jewish messianic expectations and attributes a universal significance to Jesus like that of Caesar. Koester's marshalling of references from Josephus to show that the welcome and title accorded Jesus by the Samaritans contrasts effectively to the comparable welcomes and titles accorded to Vespasian and Titus at the time of the Jewish War, p. 666, is also an extremely useful contribution.

Nevertheless, Koester's subsequent, tentative reflections regarding the influence of the colonial past of the Samaritans, pp. 675-677, and his reflections relative to the significance of a putative Samaritan membership within John's community, pp. 678-680, are considerably at variance with the line of interpretation being proposed in the present study. This criticism is not to diminish the truth of Koester's fundamental argument that the title "Savior of the world" does represent a Christian "distancing" from the cult of Rome's rulers.

21. It was indicated in chapter two that "savior of the world" was one of the titles used for Nero. As Carson, p. 232, and other commentators point out, this title was also used for Asclepius, the god of healing. The issue now being addressed is whether it was John's intention to indicate that Jesus *too* can be regarded as Savior of the world or whether Jesus *alone* can be so regarded. Carson rightly concludes that the true Savior of the world was not any god or the Roman emperor "but the

Lamb of God who takes away the sins of the world (1:29, 34)." Similarly, G. Beasley-Murray, *John* (Waco: Word Books, 1987; hereafter "Beasley-Murray"), p. 65.

22. The conclusion expressed here relative to the meaning of "Savior of the world" will be afforded additional support once the other key "Roman" terms appearing in the Gospel of John have been surveyed. "Lord" and "Lord and God" will be treated in the following section, but concepts such as "friend of Caesar" remain to be analyzed in chapters five and six. When viewed as a whole, John's Gospel can be seen to operate regarding Roman titles much in the same way that it operates relative to Jewish titles and practices. In effect (see note 17), the Gospel of John presents Jesus as fulfilling the prevailing Roman titles such as "lord," "savior of the world," and "lord and god" just as he definitely fulfills such Jewish titles as "son of man," "king of Israel," and "messiah."

23. Without explicitly recognizing the use of this title as a preeminent way for expressing faith, Schnackenburg, vol. 1, p. 508, does note that, when this form of address is used by disciples, it has a special significance. The following list serves to illustrate the extensive use of this title by the disciples closest to Jesus: Peter (6:68; 13:6,9,36-37; 21:15,16,17,21), the beloved disciple (13:25; 21:7; cf. 21:20), Mary Magdalene (20:2,13,18), Thomas (14:5), Philip (14:8), Judas not Iscariot (14:22), and "the disciples" (11:12; 20:25).

24. Examples of those who address Jesus as "Lord" while they are seemingly moving toward belief in him are the official of Capernaum (4:49), the crippled man (5:7), those who respond favorably to Jesus' bread of life discourse (6:34), and the blind man (9:36,38). The Samaritan woman herself uses this title three times (4:11,15,19).

25. As narrator John himself uses this term six times: 4:1; 6:23; 11:2; 20:20; 21:7,12. Schnackenburg, vol. 1, p. 422, is skeptical about recognizing this usage.

26. R. Bultmann. *The Gospel of John* (Philadelphia: Westminster, 1971; hereafter "Bultmann"), p. 474, holds that *ho didaskolos* and *ho kyrios* both are ways of addressing respected persons and essentially complement each other in this passage. Yet seemingly Lord has a profounder meaning here just as it does throughout the Gospel. This is perhaps also indicated by the fact that Jesus puts "Lord" ahead of "Teacher" when he formally accepts these titles in verse 14. While he himself is cautious on this point, surely Brown, vol. 2, p. 553, is correct to think that the reason why the Johannine Jesus changes the order is that "here it is a question of what he is in reality." On the subject of Jesus' sovereignty even as he acts in humble service, Lagrange, p. 355, emphasizes that Jesus maintains his dignity throughout this scene, stating: ". . . auctorité et humilité ne son pas incompatibles."

27. Carson, p. 414, emphasizes that Martha's personal trust ("Yes, Lord") and her confidence that certain things about Jesus are true (that he is the Christ, that he is the Son of God, and that he is the one who is coming into the world) are richly combined here. Schnackenburg, vol. 2, p. 332, comments extensively on the meaning of each of these last titles and stresses that "you are the Christ, the Son of God" is exactly the same combination of words that John uses in his own author's note at 20:31.

28. Brown, vol. 2, p. 1047, states, "this then is the supreme christological pronouncement of the Fourth Gospel," and comparable estimations are expressed by Barrett, p. 573, Lindars, p. 615, and Carson, p. 659. Bultmann, p. 695, provides a helpful discussion of the Old Testament instances in which terms approximate to this are used of Yahweh; he also references Suetonius' passage concerning Domi-

tian as well as the related findings indicated by Deissmann in *Light from the Ancient East*.

Bultmann does not, however, adopt a definite position as to which of these previous expressions excercised an influence upon John. Brown, vol. 2, p. 1047, mentions scholarly agreement that the frame of reference for this title as used by John is biblical, and Schnackenburg, vol. 3, p. 333, avers that a criticism of the emperor cult is scarcely to be supposed. Nevertheless, Lindars, p. 675, entertains the possibility that John had Roman imperial pretensions in mind. And such is decidedly the view of the present study: at least *in part* John was influenced by what he knew of the aggrandizing claims of one or more Roman emperors. The grounds for such a perspective regarding 20:28 are strengthened when everything else that is antithetical to the imperial cult within John's Gospel is carefully considered.

29. Carson, p. 659, states, "The repeated pronoun *my* does not diminish the universality of Jesus' lordship and deity . . . " Within the perspective of the present study, this point is an important one and should receive emphasis. For who is truly the Lord and God of the world? By Thomas' confession, it is Jesus who has this standing and, it must be stressed, Jesus alone!

The interpretation here is comparable to that advanced above in respect to the Samaritans' acclamation of Jesus as "Savior of the world." Does John envision that any deity or any Roman emperor can plausibly be considered to be Lord and God? Once such a question is asked of the text at 20:28, the answer is evident: Jesus is the only one (precluding the Father) who may be regarded in such a way. For *in reality* only Jesus has such power and such standing.

Chapter Five: The Roman Trial of Jesus

1. In the paragraphs that follow, John's presentation concerning Jesus' opponents will be analyzed in relatively general terms. In effect, what is now presented are essentially the principal insights gained at a time in this study when I considered devoting an entire chapter to the protracted conflict between Jesus and his adversaries within the Gospel. Subsequently, as I came to focus increasingly upon the consequences of the Gospel for readers challenged by their Roman circumstances, it became apparent that the opposition Jesus experienced from the chief priests and Pharisees (under Satan's influence) should be treated primarily in respect to the light that this opposition sheds upon Jesus' Roman trial.

2. The problematic subject of "the Jews" in John's Gospel has been treated extensively in the scholarly literature. Studies such as R. Fuller, "The 'Jews' in the Fourth Gospel," *Dialog* 16 (1977), pp. 31-37, and M. Shepherd, Jr., "The Jews in the Gospel of John: Another Level of Meaning," *Anglican Theological Review*, s.s. 3 (1974), pp. 95-112, have contributed to this discussion as has R. Fortna, "The Theological Use of Locale in the Fourth Gospel," pp. 85-95.

In an extremely valuable study, U. von Wahlde, "The Johannine 'Jews': A Critical Survey," *New Testament Studies* 28 (1981-82), pp. 33-60, surveys the position adopted by eleven leading scholars regarding the seventy-one instances in which John uses "the Jews" and presents his findings in a comprehensive graph. One of von Wahlde's principal conclusions—that within John's account, "the Jews" virtually always refers to the religious authorities (cf. especially pp. 45-46)—provides strong support for the position adopted here. From the standpoint of the present study, the difficulty von Walhde acknowledges with respect to the use in 6:41,52 is resolved by presuming that John understands some of the religious authorities to have been present in Galilee at the time of this episode, just as John earlier expressly states that the Pharisees sent agents to Bethany across the Jordan in order to investigate John the Baptist's activity (see 1:19-28, noting especially that 1:19 states that it was "the Jews" who sent "priests and levites").

3. The significance of this alliance will be emphasized in the paragraphs that follow. Once it is grasped that "the Jews" (negatively) are none other than the chief priests, it is clear how Annas, Caiaphas, the Sanhedrin, and ultimately Judas are a part of this group. Satan, "the ruler of this world," is also Jesus' adversary ("the world," used with negative meaning, is also a source of hostility to Jesus) and has influence over the just described alliance of Jesus' human opponents. In terms of the membership of this alliance, note that Nicodemus is a Pharisee who is portrayed positively as the Gospel moves forward (see 7:50-51; 19:39). Also, at one point some of the "the authorities" begin to believe before being intimidated by the Pharisees (see 12:42-43a).

4. "The Jews" is also frequently used by John with neutral and sometimes even with positive connotation (see 10:19; 11:33,36,45). However, what the present study is emphasizing is that, when John portrays "the Jews" acting hostilely toward Jesus, he understands members of the chief priest/Pharisee alliance to be involved. See von Wahlde, "The Johannine 'Jews': A Critical Survey," pp. 41-42, for data regarding the texts that support this conclusion.

5. This interpretation of the meaning of "the authorities" is established by reference to the context in which the term appears in 7:48 and at 12:42. The context in 7:26b is not sufficient to identify the chief priests precisely, but within John's overall framework the chief priests or the larger chief priest/Pharisee alliance can safely be presumed.

6. A full presentation concerning Satan's ominous identity in John's Gospel and the other terms John employs for him — "the devil" and "the evil one" — is beyond the scope of this study. Inasmuch as Satan is referred to as "the ruler of this world" at 12:31, 14:30, and 16:11, and inasmuch as Jesus explicitly charges that "the Jews" are "of the world" in 8:23, it can be argued that John understands (in a way it is not fully explicated) those opposing Jesus to belong to "the world" of which Satan is ruler.

Much stronger support for such an interpretation is given when 8:44 is read against the surrounding context. In 8:31ff, either some of "the Jews" have begun to believe in Jesus only to turn against him or else others of "the Jews" are understood to be present and controverting with Jesus. In either case, a sharp dispute occurs between Jesus and "the Jews," a dispute in which Jesus heatedly charges them with being related to, and supporters of, the devil: "You are of your father the devil, and your will is to do your father's desires."

7. Schnackenburg, vol. 2, pp. 346-357, provides a clear, concise discussion of the major factors to be appreciated in this passage although, clearly not all of these aspects can be adverted to here. For an in-depth, sometimes highly conjectural, and very stimulating analysis of the juridical aspects involved, see E. Bammel, *"Ex Illa Itaque Die Consilium Fecerunt . . . ,"* pp. 11-40, in *The Trial of Jesus*, ed. E. Bammel (Naperville: Allenson, 1970). On pp. 29-30, Bammel stresses that this particular session of the Sanhedrin represents the decisive action taken by Jesus' adversaries. See also A. Harvey, in *The Trial of Jesus*, p. 98.

8. Carson, p. 422, correctly assesses the thrust of Caiaphas' remarks as exhibiting the perspective of "the ruling party."

9. Haenchen, vol. 2, p. 79, is representative of a number of commentators who discuss the Old Testament (and other) precedents for the course of action articulated by Caiaphas and speculate as to whether John was familiar with them. Schnackenburg, vol. 2, p. 349, does this but then rightly emphasizes that the fundamental fact to be grasped is that Caiaphas' advice is based upon considerations of expediency. The suggestion made in the text that this is in fact a cover story arises from reflections regarding the general manipulativeness that John attributes to Jesus' adversaries in the trial before Pilate.

10. As C. H. Giblin, "Confrontations in John 18:1-27," *Biblica* 65 (1984), p. 216, observes, John portrays these Roman troops following the lead of Judas. This is a slightly startling picture given the normal anticipations of John's readers regarding the authorized deployments of Roman troops.

11. Based upon the developments that John depicts occurring outside and inside the praetorium, Brown, vol. 2, pp. 857-859, and Schnackenburg, vol. 3, pp. 220, 242, identify seven principal scenes within the "drama" of Jesus' Roman trial.

12. Barrett, p. 533, notes how John seems to assume that his readers will know who Pilate is and refers to him without any prior notice or introduction. This small point is nevertheless significant for the present thesis that John wrote for readers who were sensitive to "Roman realities."

13. *Kakon poiōn* refers to "evildoing" in general without explicitly alleging political activity. However, as observed above, Jesus' adversaries will shift charges as the trial proceeds and will eventually arrive at an explicit political accusation. Carson, p. 590, draws attention to the truculent tone of Jesus' opponents in their reply to Pilate. Pilate's own reply has overtones of arrogance and disdain.

14. Bultmann, pp. 652-653, observes that their reply makes it evident that Jesus' adversaries want nothing less than his death. In effect their reply also "constrains" Pilate — since they are pressing capital charges, he *must* become involved.

15. As just indicated, Jesus' adversaries' initial charge was generally framed. So, in effect, Pilate is trying to discover if Jesus is involved in any type of loyalty offense, any type of activity for political kingship.

16. At the conclusion of his discussion of this exchange over the release of Jesus or Barabbas, Brown observes perceptively that Pilate's position has now begun to decline: "... Pilate is reduced from a position where he could have commanded the freeing of Jesus to a position where he must bargain for it" (vol. 2, p. 872).

17. John does indeed seem to understand that Pilate was attempting to act in Jesus' interests in having him scourged and mocked. Brown, vol. 2, p. 886, notes how surprising this is.

18. Carson, pp. 599-600, discusses the various possible translations for *mallon ephobethe* and seems inclined to favor a meaning that affirms Pilate's fearfulness. D. Rensberger, *Johannine Faith and Liberating Community* (Philadelphia: Westminster, 1988), p. 94, favors the translation "he became fearful instead" on the grounds that Pilate has not been fearful up to this point. Brown, vol. 2, p. 877, favors "more afraid than ever" and discusses at some length, pp. 890-891, Pilate's growing uneasiness that he was in danger of being undermined by "the Jews."

19. Barrett, p. 543, discusses the significance of *antilegei tō Kaisari* in terms of the Roman charge of *maiestas*. Attention should also be directed to the two instances of "Caesar" within this verse (see 19:15b below for the third reference

within the Gospel). In effect, the reference point for ultimate allegiance is now introduced. Allegiance to Caesar is now explicitly set forth as the ultimate criterion for Pilate and, cynically, for Jesus' adversaries.

20. In *"Philos tou Kaisaros," Theologische Literaturzeitung* 77 (1952), pp. 205-210, E. Bammel delineates the Roman practices connected with *Amicus Caesaris* and suggests that Pilate may well have held this title. At issue then is whether John himself was aware of the official significance of this term when he included it in his account. Haenchen, vol. 2, p. 183, thinks this doubtful. Schnackenburg, vol. 3, p. 262, is more open to the possibility. Whatever John's precise awareness, what must not be overlooked is that he portrays this threat as having been absolutely decisive with Pilate. Whatever his own precise understanding, John shows unmistakably that upon hearing these words mentioned Pilate moved decisively to prevent any further publication of them!

21. In his chapter, "The Trial of Jesus and the Politics of John" in *Johannine Faith and Liberating Community*, pp. 87-106, D. Rensberger is sensitive to a number of the political implications in the interactions that comprise Jesus' Roman trial. In contrast to the present analysis, however, Rensberger interprets John's Pilate as a much more dominant figure in these proceedings, i.e., *not* as someone who is being defeated but managing to exact a price for his defeat.

22. C. H. Giblin, "John's Narration of the Hearing before Pilate (John 18:28 – 19:16a)," *Biblica* 67 (1986), p. 233, observes that Pilate's words are expressive of mock surprise: "Shall I crucify your king?" Pilate is, as Giblin states, "baiting them."

23. For an assessment of the extraordinarily demeaning character of this confession when it is viewed against the backdrop of the Passover *Haggadah's* eloquent proclamation of the kingly reign of God, see Brown, vol. 2, pp. 894-895. In his more generally framed article, "The Passion According to John: Chapters 18 and 19," *Worship* 49 (1975), p. 130, Brown provides the following concise assessment regarding Pilate's limited achievement in eliciting this confession: "The price he extracts from them by way of an insincere allegiance to Caesar (19:15) is a face-saving device for a man who knows the truth about Jesus but has failed to bear witness to it (18:37-38)."

24. As noted previously, Jesus' adversaries' opening intervention was that he was an evildoer (*kakon poiōn*) to such a degree that his execution was mandated. Pilate himself now raises the issue of subversive activity broaching the charge "king of the Jews," which Jesus' adversaries eventually used decisively against Jesus *and* Pilate.

25. As discussed by Lagrange, p. 475, it is not exactly that Jesus is assuming to be "the judge of his judge" here. Still, the boldness of his reply is remarkable. There is no sense that Jesus feels himself beholden to Pilate's power in any way. This theme of Jesus' independent (indeed, higher!) standing will be elaborated over the course of the exchanges that John will now present.

26. In his careful discussion of this passage, Rensberger, *Johannine Faith and Liberating Community*, p. 97, observes that Jesus' reply is "a declaration that Jesus' kingship has its source outside the world and so is established by methods other than those of the world." Rensberger correctly notes that Jesus' words do not deny his kingship, while "from above" in its origin, still exerts a peculiar authority over the present world. In other words, there is no certification here that Jesus' kingship is "otherworldly" in such a way as not to impinge on this world's affairs.

For an instructive discussion on the point that Jesus' reference to his *basileia* actually references his kingly *activity*, his sovereign *rule*, see Beasley-Murray, pp. 330-331.

27. "My attendants" or even "my officers" would be better renderings of *hoi hypēretai hoi emoi* in 18:36b than the *RSV*'s "my servants" is. In 18:3, the verse describing Jesus' arrest by those sent from the chief priests and Pharisees, the *RSV* translates *hypēretas* as "officers." Bultmann, p. 654, n. 4, would resolve the discussion about how Jesus can appropriately describe his disciples as *hypēretai* by understanding Jesus' statement to mean simply: "If I were a worldly king I would have *hypēretai* who would fight for me."

28. Carson, p. 595; Bultmann, p. 655.

29. Carson, p. 601, argues effectively that "power" is not what is given to Pilate from above since *exousia* is feminine while "*it* had been given" (*en dedomenon*) is neuter. Thus, in Carson's estimation, pp. 601-602, what is given to Pilate is the entire turn of events, or more precisely, the event of the betrayal itself.

30. Schnackenburg, vol. 3, p. 261, notes that, although the formulation for "delivering" to Pilate is in the singular (*ho paradous*), a general meaning is still expressed: all who have been involved in this handing over.

31. Schnackenburg, vol. 3, p. 271. Carson, pp. 610-611, remarks that by publishing a statement of the crime in these three languages, a warning was issued to every segment of the populace regarding the punishment for such activity.

32. Beasley-Murray, p. 346, assesses the proclamation made by this *titulus* as the apex of Johannine irony. Unwittingly, Pilate proclaims to Israel and to the nations that Jesus is king just as Caiaphas unwittingly prophesied that Jesus would die redemptively (11:49-50).

33. In his introductory comments to John, chapters 13 to 20, as "the Book of Glory," Brown, vol. 2, p. 541, emphasizes the triumphant element in the Johannine presentation of Jesus' crucifixion. The lifting up of the Son of man to draw all to himself, predicted at 12:32, begins on the cross where Jesus is physically lifted up from the earth. Jesus' crucifixion is not an abasement because he voluntarily lays down his life with power to take it up again, something also referred to earlier (10:18).

In her comments on the literary features of the Fourth Gospel, P. Perkins, *The Gospel According to John*. New Jerome Biblical Commentary (Englewood Cliffs: Prentice-Hall, 1990), p. 947, underscores the importance of Jesus' crucifixion as glorification in terms of the plot of John's Gospel. This plot is focused upon "the hour" of Jesus' glorification, his return to the Father at the time of his crucifixion and death. Having revealed the Father during the time of his ministry, he now returns to the "glory" that he has had previously with the Father.

34. Particularly thoughtful comments relative to Jesus' sovereignty in the circumstances of his death are given by D. M. Smith, *Johannine Christianity: Essays on Its Setting, Sources, and Theology* (Columbia: University of South Carolina, 1984), pp. 179-180.

35. Schnackenburg, vol. 3, p. 284, observes the manner in which John presents Jesus' initiatives even in these end events. Jesus takes the initiative in exhorting the beloved disciple, in the request for the final drink, and in the "rendering up" of his spirit. Carson, p. 261, comments similarly regarding the voluntary character of Jesus' death: "No one took his life from him; he had the authority to lay it down of his own accord (10:17,18), the culminating act of filial obedience (8:29; 14:31)."

36. In reflecting cautiously as to whether John understands the burial of Jesus

as a continuation of the theme of Jesus' kingship, Brown, vol. 2, p. 960, considers several factors, among them the generous amount of burial spices and the mention of burial in a garden location.

In the end, whether or not one concludes that a kingly burial is implied depends to a considerable degree upon how much weight is given to John's consistent presentation of Jesus' sovereignty up until this point. Haenchen's statement in this regard, vol. 2, p. 202, while true, is probably too minimal: "It is designed to persuade the believer that God's gracious plan, conceived long ago, is being fulfilled here, and that Jesus, in spite of everything, received an honorable burial and not the ignominious end of a law breaker."

Chapter Six: Jesus' Farewell Discourses

1. Within the text the factors indicating persecution at the hands of religious authorities are the following. First, in 16:2b Jesus seemingly adverts to a religious motive for the lethal persecution he foresees (also, the expulsion from the synagogue that he refers to in 16;2a would obviously be carried out by religious officials). Second, inasmuch as the agents of Jesus' own persecution were the chief priests and Pharisees, his prediction in 15:20 that the disciples will experience similar persecution implies that this will also come from the religious authorities. Third, when Jesus states to the disciples that they will be "scattered," and in the world have persecution (16:32-33), it soon emerges that they are literally scattered as the result of Jesus' arrest, ordered and accomplished by his religious adversaries.

While the line of approach followed in the present study does not require that there be a reference to political persecution in these persecution passages, it should still be noted that Jesus' references to the hatred of "the world" for his disciples (15:18-19) provides at least some basis for the interpretation that other types of persecution in addition to religious persecution are envisioned.

Additionally it is possible that the killing mentioned in 16:2b could encompass the idea of executions by political authorities. While favoring the interpretation that the persecution of Christians by Jewish authorities is the meaning here, Brown does include the following statement in his discussion of this passage: "We are told that at a slightly later period Trajan's gratitude to the gods for victories over the Dacians and Scythians led him to persecute the Christians who refused to acknowledge these gods" (vol. 2, p. 691).

2. The analysis made by J. L. Martyn, *History and Theology in the Fourth Gospel* (Nashville: Abingdon, 1979), has been influential in the contemporary discussion of the Johannine persecution passages. In effect, Martyn holds for two types of persecution by the Jewish authorities. Exclusion from the synagogue that was accomplished through the *Birkat-ha-Minim*, an addition to the Twelfth of the Eighteen Benedictions, represented one stage of persecution (pp. 50-62, 156-157). In addition, there were aggressive measures against Christians to the point of killing (pp. 72, 81).

In focusing explicitly on the principal persecution passage in John, B. Lindars, "The Persecution of Christians in John 15:18 — 16:4a," *Suffering and Martyrdom in the New Testament* (Cambridge: Cambridge University Press, 1981), also envisions the Jewish authorities proceeding in these two ways against Christians. Following Martyn on the use of the *Birkat-ha-Minim* for exclusionary purposes (p. 49), Lindars also envisions the situation in which Jewish officials went beyond exclusion to violent even fanatical persecution (p. 67).

In the first chapters of his study *The Theme of Jewish Persecution of Christians in the Gospel According to St. Matthew* (Cambridge: Cambridge University Press, 1967), D. Hare's assessment of the actual historical situation for Jews and Christians during this period is sharply in tension with the historical situation envisioned by both Martyn and Lindars. Hare argues against interpreting the *Birkat-ha-Minim* as directed against Christians (p. 59). His findings with respect to lethal persecution are as follows: "We have discovered no clear instance of execution of Christians by Jewish religious authorities for purely religious reasons. There is no evidence of a systematic effort to eliminate Christianity by treating it as a capital crime" (p. 42).

3. Carson, p. 530, comments that apostasy, not death, is the greatest danger that the disciples face.

4. Brown, vol. 1, pp. 510-512, provides an instructive overview of how John uses *menein* to express the permanency and the reciprocity in the relationship between the Father and Jesus and between Jesus and his disciples.

5. Carson, pp. 510-511, provides a clear analysis of how 15:9-16 recapitulates some of the key themes of the vine and branches image of 15:1-8. At the same time the vine and branches metaphor enriches the exposition given in 15:9-16.

6. Barrett, p. 476, comments that the death of Jesus is at once the unsurpassed expression of eternal divine love and the death of a man for his friends. Addressing the objection that self-sacrificing love for enemies is greater than self-sacrificing love for friends, Carson, p. 522 responds that, in this context, Jesus is addressing friends and is concerned to lay out a pattern for *their* future behavior.

7. The translation used for these four verses and for 15:13 later in this section is that of the *New Revised Standard Version*.

8. When this verse is regarded in connection with 15:9a, "As the Father has loved me, so I have loved you," it emerges that the disciples exist in what D. Harrington, *John's Thought and Theology* (Collegeville: Liturgical Press, 1990), p. 90, calls "a chain of love." Given the hatred by "the world" described in 15:21-25, Harrington remarks, p. 91, that the disciples also experience "a chain of hatred."

An additional sharp contrast between the situation that the disciples have with Jesus as opposed to that offered by "the world" is given by Jesus' words "Peace I leave with you, my peace I give you; not as the world gives do I give you ... " (14:27). This contrast is also to be seen in Jesus' previously analyzed reply to Pilate indicating that his kingship is not of this world (18:36). Indeed, taking these two references together it can be hypothesized that John may have consciously been concerned to distinguish Jesus' peace and kingship from the *Pax Romana* presided over by the Roman emperors. For not according to the practices of these emperors does John's Jesus give his peace.

9. The analysis of Satan's role made in the text and the notes of chapter five, section one, should be recalled in this context.

10. For an analysis of the place of the Holy Spirit within the Fourth Gospel as a whole, see Barrett, pp. 88-92. For an extended, in-depth treatment of the Paraclete passages in the farewell discourses, see (in addition to his comments ad loc.) Schnackenburg's excursus, "The Paraclete and Sayings about the Paraclete," in vol. 3, pp. 138-154.

11. Schnackenburg, vol. 3, p. 139; Barrett, p. 462.

12. Schnackenburg, vol. 3, p. 117, notes that the Paraclete, as Jesus' witness,

does not speak to the world directly, but rather makes use of the disciples to do this. He comments further, p. 118, "The witness borne by the Paraclete and that borne by the disciples are expressed in two separate sentences placed side by side, but they come together to form a single witness." Additionally, relevant is Schnackenburg's comment on p. 119: "The saying about the Paraclete ... belongs closely to the idea of the hatred of the world and the persecution that the disciples have to endure for Jesus' sake. It also points forward to 16:8-11, in which the activity of the Paraclete with regard to the world as a legal procedure is described."

13. A. Harvey, *Jesus on Trial*, p. 115, states the following in regard to the Paraclete's defending prosecuting roles: "In particular, the inevitable figure of an advocate — a *paraclete* — can be shown also to be already active on earth, in the person of the Holy Spirit, defending and accusing. And these activities the Spirit combines with others already experienced in the Christian Church (and partly understood already in Judaism) such as guiding, teaching, inspiring, and foretelling ... "

14. Overview reflections about the character of the Roman persecution of Christians given by A. N. Sherwin-White in his study *The Letters of Pliny* were cited above in note 9 and note 24 for chapter three. In this context it is appropriate to cite the general assessment that Sherwin-White offers in his essay "The Trial of Christ," in *Historicity and Chronology in the New Testament* (London: SPCK, 1965), p. 116. Indeed the assessment given there provides significant additional support for the present study's thesis that Roman persecution was a factor impinging upon some of John's readers and John himself: "It is precisely in the second generation of the Church's life that there emerged in the eastern provinces an organized technique of persecution, though its active excercise was sporadic and occasional. This technique was fully established, according to the letter of Pliny about the Christians of Pontus, by the period A.D. 90-110, and its beginnings date back to the first anti-Christian action at Rome under Nero in A.D. 64."

15. A. Harvey, *Jesus on Trial*, p. 107, draws attention to the possibility that the Christian belief of John's readers could have placed them in jeopardy from both Jewish and Roman sources. In the latter part of the comment now to be cited, Harvey is reflecting again upon the Paraclete's role in assisting these beleaguered Christians; however, in this instance, it is his initial reflection that merits the use of italics: "They must expect to appear on trial because of their religion, *both in Jewish and in pagan courts*; but they would find they were not alone, and their defense would not depend only on their own ingenuity."

The present thesis concerning the possibility that roughly contemporaneous religious and political persecutions *both* affected John's readers does not preclude the possibility that persecution by the Roman authorities might have occurred after these Christians had been expelled from the synagogue and might have been a consequence of this expulsion. Nevertheless, with respect to all scenarios positing Jewish persecution, the skepticism expressed by D. Hare as to the reliability of the empirical data attesting to such persecution must be born in mind (see note 2 above and indeed Hare's entire discussion in the first two chapters of *Themes of Jewish Persecution in the Gospel According to St. Matthew*).

16. In this instance and circumstance, as Schnackenburg observes, vol. 3, p. 109, there is a certain narrowing of the teaching on love to the circle of the disciples. However, it should not be thought that John's overall description of Jesus' ministry is without instances of outreach beyond this inner circle. For a stimulating study in

this regard, see. R. Karris, *Jesus and the Marginalized in John's Gospel* (Collegeville: Liturgical Press, 1990).

17. Because his suggested interpretations pertain to 15:18—16:4a as a whole, it has seemed wise to postpone the treatment of F. Vouga's views until the full analysis of the present chapter had been completed. Summarizing, it can be seen that in his study, *La cadre historique et l'intention théologique de Jean* (Paris: Beauschesne, 1977), Vouga, pp. 106-111, discusses John 15:18-16:4a principally in terms of three hypotheses: (a) that the Johannine community was mistakenly the victim of anti-semitism; (b) that it was the victim of imperial absolutism; and (c) that it was the victim of the municipal patriotism of cities within the provinces. On pp. 108-110, in his discussion of his second hypothesis, Vouga is sensitive to the possibility that persecution under Domitian could have been an influence upon the Gospel and this sensitivity is to be affirmed.

However, in the main, Vouga locates John's response to this persecution in the trial narrative of the Gospel and comments upon this narrative largely in terms of the traditional "political apologetic" theory, i.e., John portrays Jesus interacting with Pilate in such a way as to minimize imperial suspicions regarding Christianity. For a critique of the political apologetic purpose usually ascribed to Luke, see respectively R. Cassidy, *Jesus, Politics and Society: A Study of Luke's Gospel* (Mary-knoll, New York: Orbis Books, 1978) pp. 7-9, 128-130, and *Society and Politics in the Acts of the Apostles* (Maryknoll, New York: Orbis Books, 1987) pp. 145-155. Although a full discussion obviously cannot be undertaken at this point, my own previous work in this area and the analysis that I have made in the preceding chapter of this study have convinced me that John does not advance a political apologetic in his trial narrative any more than Luke does.

In addition, reservations must be expressed about the decisive influence that Vouga ascribes to Jewish opponents of the Johannine community. His principal suggestion at this point is that John 16:2b refers to the efforts by Jews to have the Roman authorities act as "intermediaries" in accomplishing the death of Christians. Thus, according to Vouga, synagogue officials expelled Christians in order to deprive them of their *religio licita* standing and then, at the time of Domitian, incited the Roman authorities to act directly against these Christians.

In summary, from the perspective of the present study Vouga's sensitivity to the possibility that persecutions under Domitian may have influenced John's Gospel is to be affirmed. However, his political apologetic interpretation of John's response to such persecution is surely incorrect. And his suggestion that hatred by Jews was a key factor influencing any imperial persecutions must be viewed with extreme caution in light of the conclusions reached by D. Hare in his study of this period (see notes 2 and 15 above).

Chapter Seven: John 20-21 and Readers in Roman Surroundings

1. Scholars who argue that John 21 was added by someone other than the writer of chapters 1-20 (this view is adopted by a significant majority of scholars) generally cite both linguistic/stylistic features and theological factors in support of their position. See, for example, Barrett, pp. 576-577; Schnackenburg, vol. 3, pp. 341-344; Haenchen, vol. 2, pp. 229-230; and the detailed discussion provided by Brown, vol. 2, pp. 1077-1080.

Representatives from the much smaller group of scholars who make the interpretation that John 21 is from the same hand responsible for chapters 1-20 include Lagrange, p. cxx, p. 534; Lindars, p. 622 (tentatively); Carson, pp. 665-668; S. Smalley, "The Sign in John 21," *New Testament Studies* 20 (1974), pp. 275-288; H. Thyen, "Entwicklungen innerhalb der johanneischen Theologie und Kirche im Spiegel von Joh. 21 und der Lieblingsjüngertexte des Evangeliums," *L'Évangile de Jean: Sources, rédaction, théologie* (Gembloux: Duculot, 1977), pp. 259-299; and P. Minear, "The Original Functions of John 21," *Journal of Biblical Literature* 102 (1983), pp. 85-98.

2. Once the subject of the sources for John's Gospel is explicitly broached, the discussion of the process by which the Gospel reached its final form becomes immensely more complicated. The subject of sources was briefly referred to in note 4 for chapter one when it was mentioned that preached homilies might have been utilized as a source. Within Johannine studies a discussion regarding a "signs source," actively conducted since the time of Bultmann's commentary, received further stimulation from the publication of R. Fortna's *The Gospel of Signs* (Cambridge: Cambridge University Press, 1970). For a clear summary of the leading contemporary approaches regarding John's sources and traditions, see Beasley-Murray, pp. xxxviii-xliii.

3. That all of the existing manuscripts include John 21 is observed by Lindars, p. 618, and emphasized by Carson, p. 667. Brown, vol. 2, p. 1077, states: "From textual evidence including that of such early witnesses as P-66 and Tertullian, the Gospel was never circulated without ch. xxi." In the same vein, in "The Original Functions of John 21," p. 86, P. Minear writes: "Considering this evidence, we must presume that the Gospel *never* in fact appeared without this present conclusion."

4. Again, within the present study, the decision taken to circulate the Gospel is viewed as having foundational importance. This decision determined finally what would be included and what would be omitted from the text to be published. As indicated in chapter one above, *John* is understood to be the person who was responsible for the text at this point. After observing that there are aspects of canonicity involved, C. K. Barrett reemphasizes his own view of the author of the Gospel as " 'the man (or group) who would accept responsibility for the book as we read it in the ancient MSS.' *Someone* published it substantially as it now stands . . ." (p. 22).

5. The principal consideration here is that Jesus' words emphasize belief and indeed belief without seeing. Both of these aspects prepare the way for John's author's note in which he encourages his readers (who do not have the benefit of seeing) to believe.

6. An additional work emphasizing John's high christology, although not in terms of its implications for Roman persecution, is appropriately cited here. J. Neyrey, *An Ideology of Revolt: John's Christology in Social Science Perspective* (Minneapolis: Fortress, 1988) analyzes the implications of John's christology as an "ideology of revolt" against synagogue Judaism and other forms of Christian confession.

7. Carson, p. 661.

8. For additional reflections concerning the significance that John may have attached to this phrase, see section four below.

9. For an analysis of the various levels of meaning present in the episode concerning the miraculous catch of fish in 21:1-14, see R. Pesch, *Der reiche Fischfang (Lk 5:1-11/Jo 21:1-14)* (Dusseldorf: Patmos, 1969).

10. For a concise, well-presented analysis of Jesus' conversation with Peter in 21:15-17, see Beasley-Murray, pp. 404-407. With respect to the nuances present in Jesus' questions and Peter's replies, see the notes provided by Brown, vol. 2, pp. 1102-1106. See also Brown's extended comment on the general significance of Jesus' commission, pp. 1112-1117. For an analysis that emphasizes how well integrated John's presentation of Peter in chapter 21 is with his presentation of him earlier in the Gospel, see P. Minear, *John: The Martyr's Gospel*, pp. 153-162.

11. Lindars, pp. 636-637; Barrett, p. 585; and Haenchen, vol. 2, pp. 226-227, 232-233 are among those scholars who see a reference to crucifixion in this verse. In moving to his own conclusion that Peter's martyrdom is indicated, Haenchen provides a helpful discussion of the nuances of meaning present in the pairs of words and phrases in 21:18-19a.

12. With John's narrator's comment thereby confirming Peter's fate of martyrdom by crucifixion, a further dimension of John's meaning deserves emphasis at this point. It is the meaning that martyrdom through crucifixion is unalterably martyrdom at the hands of the Roman authorities. For in the context in which John's Gospel is situated who else but Roman officials have the capability for executing in this way? This point must be stressed because of the influence of the interpretation that John envisions Jewish synagogue officials subjecting Christians to martyrdom (for the express view that Jewish authorities, after expelling Christians from the synagogue, then inflicted a "second trauma" upon them by subjecting them to trial and execution as "ditheists," see J. L. Martyn, "Glimpses into the History of the Johannine Community," in *L'Évangile de Jean: sources, rédaction, théologie*, p. 162. Clearly, in presenting Peter's manner of death, John does not advert to any involvement by synagogue officials but rather envisions the decisive intervention of the Roman authorities. Again crucifixion in John's setting is undeniably a Roman prerogative.

13. P. Minear, *John: The Martyr's Gospel*, pp. 157-159, argues that there is a connection between Jesus' injunction to Peter here and the conversation between Jesus and Peter at the time of the final supper (13:36-38). John there portrays Jesus asserting that Peter was unable to follow him *at that time*, but that, afterward, he would follow him. Minear's point thus is that the future fulfillment of this prediction is now adverted to just as Jesus' other prediction that Peter would deny him three times was fulfilled at the time of his passion.

Clearly Minear brings commendable sensitivity to his analysis of John's presentation of Peter in chapter 21. For completeness it should be noted that, somewhat surprisingly, Minear does not advert to the fact of Peter's death as *Roman* martyrdom. The general theme of his book is rather that, throughout his Gospel, John portrays *Jesus* as a martyr, that is, one who witnesses and one who gives faithful testimony even to the point of laying down his life. This general theme of *witness* is, indeed, a rich theme within John's Gospel and exegetically has been treated thoroughly by J. Beutler in *Martyria: Traditionsgeschichtliche Untersuchungen zum Zeugnisthema bei Johannes* (Frankfurt: Knecht, 1972).

14. In contrast with the significant conversation between Jesus and Peter at 18:36-38, here the setting is casual and relaxed, a post-breakfast walk seemingly along the edge of the lake. Peter is also portrayed as very much at peace with Jesus here. He does not ask about Jesus' future mode of being or about his own future, although Jesus reminds him that he will have enough to do with his own discipleship.

It is thus within a cordial context that Peter ventures to bring up the subject of what will happen to another.

15. Schnackenburg, vol. 3, p. 368, notes that the narrator concentrates a positive light upon this disciple at 21:20 by indicating again that this disciple was beloved by Jesus and by "flashing back" to the last supper scene in which this disciple was especially trusted by Jesus. Schnackenburg then observes that Peter's question itself engenders the expectation that there must indeed be something special about this man. (For the sake of completeness, it should be noted that Schnackenburg expresses mild criticism about the literary technique, or lack thereof, by which the beloved disciple is introduced at this juncture.)

16. Schnackenburg discusses this question in vol. 1, pp. 202-204, and moves to a full, revised assessment in his excursus, "The Disciple Whom Jesus Loved," vol. 3, pp. 375-388. Brown's own revised assessment is provided in his work *The Community of the Beloved Disciple* (Mahwah, New Jersey: Paulist Press, 1979), pp. 31-34. A particularly lucid discussion of the presentation of the beloved disciple in John 21:20-24 is given by Beasley-Murray, pp. 409-415.

17. The Greek indicates the emphatic character of Jesus' command. Here *sy moi akolouthei*; at 21:19, *akoluthei moi*. Beasley-Murray, p. 410, suggests the following translation as a means of indicating the force of Jesus' words: "As for you, *you follow me*."

18. Additional reflections on the complementarity of Peter and the beloved disciple will be presented in the following section.

19. P. Minear, "The Original Functions of John 21," pp. 87-90, advances the view that the author's note of 20:30-31 is written as a conclusion for the material contained in chapter 20 rather than for the entire preceding Gospel. In particular, Minear asserts that the "signs done in the presence of the disciples" of 20:30 is a reference to the four episodes of chapter 20 in which strategic visions are followed by the disciples' belief or unbelief. Minear also discusses, pp. 97-98, the precise relation between 20:30-31 and 21:25, suggesting that, at the end of chapter 20, John was concerned to help his readers make the shift from the faith of the first disciples to their own faith, which could not be based upon seeing. Then, at the end of chapter 21, having (among other things) explicated the life course of two prominent disciples, John again addressed his readers directly, urging them to continue believing in Jesus, presumably in the new situation that was present after the original apostles had died. Minear states that he advances these interpretations knowing full well that "the jury of modern NT scholars has agreed with unparalleled unaminity on one issue in Johannine research: chapter 21 is not an integral part of the original gospel but was composed separately and probably by a redactor" (p. 85).

20. It is perhaps worth noting that such powerful acclamations as "my Lord and my God" and "Jesus, savior of the world" could conceivably have been useful as expressions of encouragement at the time of trial or even at the time of martyrdom.

21. It is thus not required for the validity of the present thesis that John's readers actually be in the midst of persecution. If persecution had occurred earlier, if it had only occurred in one part of the empire, or if events were taking place that rendered persecution a distinct possibility in the future, John's inclusion of material indicating that Jesus predicted Peter's death at Roman hands would have been highly instructive.

22. P. Minear, "The Original Functions of John 21," p. 95, sees 21:24-25 as placing the beloved disciple in high profile as a faithful transmitter of the tradition

of faith. R. Culpepper, *The Anatomy of the Fourth Gospel*, pp. 122-123, calls attention to the remarkable similarities between the role ascribed to the Holy Spirit
(Paraclete) and that delineated for the beloved disciple. For example, the Paraclete
was to remain with the disciples (14:7) and bring to remembrance everything that
Jesus had taught (14:26).

For perspective on the truth and believability that are characteristics of the
beloved disciple's witness here, see J. Beutler's section, *"Martyria Alēthēs,"* in his
Martyria, pp. 231-232. As is well known, the meaning of "we know" in 21:24b is
widely controverted. (See also the discussion in the various commentaries regarding
the "we" usage at 1:1-14 and at other places in the Gospel.) Interpreting this
concluding note as given by a single person. J. Sanders, *A Commentary on the Gospel
According to St. John* (London: Black 1968), p. 48, suggests that this "we know" is
an instance of an author taking readers into confidence and assuming that they
share the author's opinion.

23. Bultmann's view, p. 716, that the beloved disciple's remaining is presented
as more advantageous and, much less, his suggestion that the beloved disciple takes
Peter's place inasmuch as Peter is called to martyrdom, p. 717, scarcely can be
gleaned from the text. See Beasley-Murray's criticism of such interpretations, p.
410. Beasley-Murray's own assessment is the following: "So the author endeavored
to show that both men were gifts of the risen Lord to the churches, very different
in gifts and calling, but with important tasks to perform for the benefit of all" (p.
411).

Selected Bibliography

I. Sources and Studies Pertaining to Christianity and Roman Rule

Arnold, W. T. *The Roman System of Provincial Administration.* Oxford: Blackwell, 1914.

Baron, S. *A Social and Religious History of the Jews.* New York: Columbia University Press, 1952.

Barrett C. K., ed. *The New Testament Background.* New York: Macmillan, 1957.

Benko, S. *Pagan Rome and the Early Christians.* Bloomington, Indiana: University of Indiana Press, 1984.

Brown, R., and Meier, J. *Antioch and Rome.* New York: Paulist Press, 1983.

Bousset, W. *Kyrios Christos.* Translated by J. Steely. Nashville: Abingdon, 1970.

Buchler, A. "On the History of the Temple Worship in Jerusalem." In *Studies in Jewish History*, pp. 24-63. Edited by I. Brodie and J. Rabbinowitz. New York: Oxford University Press, 1956.

————. "The Priestly Dues and the Roman Taxes in the Edicts of Caesar." In *Studies in Jewish History*, pp. 1-23. Edited by I. Brodie and J. Rabbinowitz. New York: Oxford University Press, 1956.

Cassidy, R. *Jesus, Politics and Society: A Study of Luke's Gospel.* Maryknoll, New York: Orbis Books, 1978.

————. *Society and Politics in the Acts of the Apostles.* Maryknoll, New York: Orbis Books, 1987.

————. "Matthew 17:24-27 — a Word on Civil Taxes," *Catholic Biblical Quarterly* 41 (1979), pp. 571-580.

Charlesworth, M. "The Flavian Dynasty," *Cambridge Ancient History* 11. New York: Macmillan, 1936.

————. "Some Observations on Ruler-Cult Especially in Rome," *Harvard Theological Review* 28 (1935), pp. 5-44.

Daube, D. *Appeasement or Resistance and Other Essays on New Testament Judaism.* Berkeley, California: University of California Press, 1987.

————. *Civil Disobedience in Antiquity.* Edinburgh: Edinburgh University Press, 1972.

————. *The New Testament and Rabbinic Judaism.* London: University of London, 1956.

————. *Studies in Biblical Law.* Cambridge: Cambridge University Press, 1947.

Deissmann, A. *Bible Studies.* Translated by A. Grieve Edinburgh: Clark, 1901

————. *Light from the Ancient East.* 4th ed. Translated by L. Strachan. Grand Rapids: Baker, 1965, reprint.

Dio Cassius. *Roman History.* Translated by E. Cary. New York: Loeb Classical Library, 1914.

Dio Chrysostom. *The Orations*. Translated by H. Crosby. Cambridge, Massachusetts: Loeb Classical Library, 1946.

Duckworth, H. "The Roman Provincial System." In *The Beginnings of Christianity, 1:171-217*. Edited by F. Jackson and K. Lake. London: Macmillan, 1920.

Elliott, J. H. *A Home for the Homeless: A Sociological Exegesis of I Peter, Its Situation and Strategy*. Minneapolis: Fortress, 1981.

Eusebius. *The Ecclesiastical History and the Martyrs of Palestine*. 2 vols. Translated by H. Lawlor and J. Oulton. London: SPCK, 1927-28.

Frend, W. *Martyrdom and Persecution in the Early Church*. Grand Rapids: Baker, 1981, reprint.

Goppelt, L. *Apostolic and Post-Apostolic Times*. Translated by R. Buelich. London: Black, 1970.

Grant, R. *Augustus to Constantine*. New York: Harper & Row, 1970.

————. *The Sword and the Cross*. New York: Macmillan, 1955.

Guterman, S. L. *Religious Toleration and Persecution in Ancient Rome*. London: Aiglon, 1951.

Hardy, E. G. *Christianity and the Roman Empire*. New York: Macmillan, 1925.

Hare, D. *The Theme of Jewish Persecution of Christians in the Gospel According to St. Matthew*. Cambridge: Cambridge University Press, 1967.

Hart, H.S.J. "Judea and Rome: the Official Commentary," *Journal of Theological Studies*, N.S. vol. 3, pt. 2 (1952), pp. 172-204.

Higgins, A.J. "Sidelight on Christian Beginnings in the Graeco-Roman World," *Evangelical Quarterly* 41 (1969), pp. 197-206.

Irenaeus. *Adversus Haereses*. Translated by J. Smith. Westminster, Maryland: Newman, 1952.

Josephus. *Jewish Antiquities*. Translated by H. Thackeray et al. New York: Loeb Classical Library, 1930.

————. *The Jewish War*. Translated by H. Thackeray. New York: Loeb Classical Library, 1926.

Keresztes, P. "The Jews, the Christians, and Emperor Domitian," *Vigilae Christianae* 27 (1973), pp. 1-28.

Magie, D. *Roman Rule in Asia Minor*. 2 vols. Princeton: Princeton University Press, 1950.

Martial. *Epigrams*. Translated by W. Ker. Cambridge, Massachusetts: Loeb Classical Library, 1947.

Mattingly, H. *Coins of the Roman Empire in the British Museum* 3. London: Trustees of the British Museum, 1966.

Mommsen, T. *The Provinces of the Roman Empire*. 2 vols. Translated by W. Dickson. New York: Scribner's, 1906.

————. *Romisches Staatsrecht*. 3 vols. Leipzig: Hirzel, 1887.

Moore, G. *Judaism in the First Centuries of the Christian Era* 2. Cambridge, Massachusetts: Harvard University Press, 1927.

Philo. *The Embassy to Gaius*. Translated by F. Colson. New York: Loeb Classical Library, 1942.

Pliny. *Letters and Panegyricus*. Translated by B. Radice. Cambridge, Massachusetts: Loeb Classical Library, 1969.

Price, S. *Rituals and Power: The Roman Imperial Cult in Asia Minor*. Cambridge: Cambridge University Press, 1984.

Rostovtzeff, M. *The Social and Economic History of the Roman Empire*. Oxford: Clarendon Press, 1957.

Sandmel, S. *The First Century in Judaism and Christianity: Certainties and Uncertainties*. New York: Oxford University Press, 1969.

Schille, G. *Das vorysynoptische Judenchristentum*. Stuttgart: Calwer, 1970.

Scramuzza, V.M. "The Policy of the Early Roman Emperors Towards Judaism." In *The Beginnings of Christianity, 5:277-297* Edited by F. Jackson and K. Lake. London: Macmillan, 1933.

Scott, K. "The Elder and Younger Pliny on Emperor Worship," *Transactions of the American Philological Association* 63 (1932), pp. 156-165.

Sherwin-White, A. N. *Fifty Letters of Pliny*. Oxford: Oxford University Press, 1967.

———. *The Letters of Pliny: a Historical and Social Commentary*. Oxford: Clarendon, 1966.

———. *Roman Society and Roman Law in the New Testament*. Oxford: Clarendon Press, 1963.

Sordi, M. *The Christians in the Roman Empire*. Translated by A. Bedini. Norman, Oklahoma: University of Oklahoma Press, 1986.

Spence-Jones, H. *The Early Christians in Rome*. London: Methuen, 1910.

Stauffer, E. *Jerusalem und Rom im Zeitalter Jesu Christi*. Bern: Francke, 1957.

Suetonius. *The Lives of the Caesars*. Translated by J. Rolfe. Cambridge, Massachusetts: Loeb Classical Library, 1914.

Stevenson, G. H. *Roman Provincial Administration*. Oxford: Blackwell, 1949.

Tacitus. *The Annals*. Translated by J. Jackson. New York: Loeb Classical Library, 1942.

———. *The Histories*. Translated by C. Moore. New York: Loeb Classical Library, 1925-31.

Tcherikover, V., and A. Kuks, eds. *Corpus Papyrorum Judicarum* 2. Cambridge, Massachusetts: Harvard University Press, 1960.

Waters, K. "The Character of Domitian," *Phoenix* 18 (1964), pp. 49-77.

Workman, H. *Persecution in the Early Church*. London: Sharp, 1923.

II. Studies Interpreting John's Gospel

Bammel, E. "Ex Illa Itaque Die Consilium Fecerunt. . . ." In *The Trial of Jesus*, pp. 11-40. Edited by E. Bammel Naperville, Illinois: Allenson, 1970.

———. "Philos tou Kaisaros," *Theologische Literaturzeitung* 77 (1952), pp. 205-210.

Barrett, C. K. *Essays on John*. London: SPCK, 1982.

———. *The Gospel According to St. John*. 2d ed. Philadelphia: Westminster, 1978.

Beasley-Murray, G. *John*. Word Bible Commentary. Waco, Texas: Word Books, 1987.

Beutler, J. *Martyria. Traditionsgeschichtliche Untersuchungen zum Zeugnisthema bei Johannes*. Frankfurt: Knecht, 1972.

———. and R. Fortna, eds. *The Shepherd Discourse in John 10 and Its Context*. Cambridge: Cambridge University Press, 1991.

———. "Greeks Come to See Jesus (John 12:20f)," *Biblica* 71 (1990), pp. 333-47.

———. "Die Heilsbedeutung des Todes Jesu im Johannesevangelium nach Joh 13:1-20." In *Der Tod Jesu*, pp. 188-204. Edited by K. Kertelge. Freiburg: Herder, 1976.

Boismard, M-E. "Un procede redactionnel dans le quatrieme evangile: la Wiederaufnahme." In *L'Évangile de Jean*, pp. 235-241. Edited by M. deJonge. Gembloux: Duculot, 1977.

Braun, F. M. *Jean le Théologien*. 2 vols. Paris: Gabalda, 1959-1964.

Brown, R. *The Community of the Beloved Disciple*. Mahwah, New Jersey: Paulist Press, 1979.

————. *The Gospel According to John*. 2 vols. Garden City, New York: Doubleday, 1966-71.

————. *The Gospel and Epistles of John: A Concise Commentary*. Collegeville: Liturgical Press, 1988.

————. "The Passion According to John: Chapters 18 and 19," *Worship* 49 (1975), pp. 126-134.

Bruce, F. F. *The Gospel of John*. Grand Rapids, Michigan: Eerdmans, 1983.

Bultmann, R. *The Gospel of John*. Philadelphia: Westminster, 1971.

Carson, D. A. *The Gospel According to John*. Grand Rapids: 1991.

————. "John and the Johannine Epistles." In *It is Written: Scripture Citing Scripture*, pp. 245-264. Edited by D. A. Carson and J. Williamson. Cambridge: Cambridge University Press, 1988.

Collins, R. *These Things Have Been Written: Studies on the Fourth Gospel*. Grand Rapids: Eerdmans, 1990.

Countryman, W. *The Mystical Way in the Fourth Gospel*. Minneapolis: Fortress, 1987.

Cullman, O. *The Johannine Circle*. Translated by J. Bowden. London: SCM, 1976.

Culpepper, R. *Anatomy of the Fourth Gospel: A Study in Literary Design*. Minneapolis: Fortress, 1983.

de la Potterie, I. *The Hour of Jesus: The Passion and Resurrection of Jesus According to St. John*. Translated by G. Murray. New York: Alba House, 1989.

————. *La Vérité dans Saint Jean*. 2 vols. Rome: Biblical Institute Press, 1977.

————. "Parole et esprit dans S. Jean." In *L'Évangile de Jean*, pp. 177-201. Edited by M. deJonge. Gembloux: Duculot, 1977.

Dodd, C. H. *History and Tradition in the Fourth Gospel*. Cambridge: Cambridge University Press, 1953.

————. *The Interpretation of the Fourth Gospel*. Cambridge: Cambridge University Press, 1953.

Duke, P. *Irony in the Fourth Gospel*. Atlanta: Knox, 1985.

Fenton, J. *The Gospel According to John*. Oxford: Clarendon: 1970.

Fortna, R. *The Fourth Gospel and Its Predecessor*. Minneapolis: Fortress, 1988.

————. *The Gospel of Signs*. Cambridge: Cambridge University Press, 1970.

————. "Theological Use of Locale in the Fourth Gospel," *Anglican Theological Review*, Supplementary Series 3 (1974), pp. 58-95.

Fuller, R. "The 'Jews' in the Fourth Gospel," *Dialog* 16 (1977), pp. 31-37.

Giblin, C. H. "Confrontations in John 18:1-27," *Biblica* 65 (1984), pp. 210-231.

————. "John's Narration of the Hearing before Pilate (John 18:28-19:16a)," *Biblica* 67 (1986), pp. 221-239.

————. "Suggestion, Negative Response, and Positive Action in St. John's Portrayal of Jesus," *New Testament Studies* 26 (1979-80), pp. 197-211.

————. "The Tripartite Narrative Structure of John's Gospel," *Biblica Literature* 109 (1990), pp. 665-680.

Gnilka, J. *Johannesevangelium*. Wurzburg: Echter, 1983.

Haenchen, E. *A Commentary on the Gospel of John*. Translated by R. Funk. 2 vols. Minneapolis: Fortress, 1984.

Harrington, D. *John's Thought and Theology: An Introduction* Collegeville: Liturgical Press, 1990.

Hartman, L., and B. Olsson, eds. *Aspects on the Johannine Literature*. Upsala: Coniectanea Biblica, NTS 18, 1987.

Harvey, A. *Jesus on Trial: A Study in the Fourth Gospel*. London: SCM, 1976.

Hoskyns, E. *The Fourth Gospel*. 2d ed. Edited by F. Davey. London: Faber and Faber, 1947.

deJonge, M., ed. *L'Évangile de Jean: Sources, rédaction théologie*. Gembloux: Duculot, 1977.

Karris, R. *Jesus and the Marginalized in John's Gospel*. Collegeville: Liturgical Press, 1990.

Koester, C. " 'The Savior of the World' (John 4:42)," *Journal of Biblical Literature* 109 (1990), pp. 665-680.

Kysar, R. *The Fourth Evangelist and His Gospel: An Examination of Contemporary Scholarship*. Minneapolis: Augsburg, 1975.

———. *John*. Minneapolis: Augsburg, 1986.

———. *John, the Maverick Gospel*. Atlanta: Knox, 1976.

Lagrange, M-J. *Évangile selon Saint Jean*. Paris: Gabalda, 1936.

Lindars, B. *The Gospel of John*. Grand Rapids: Eerdmans, 1972.

———. "The Persecution of Christians in John 15:18-16:4a." In *Suffering and Martyrdom in the New Testament*, pp. 48-69. Edited by W. Horbury and B. McNeil. Cambridge: Cambridge University Press, 1981.

Marsh, J. *The Gospel of St. John*. Harmondsworth: Penguin, 1968.

Martini, C. *Il Vangelo Secondo Giovanni*. Rome: Borla, 1979.

Martyn, J. L. *History and Theology in the Fourth Gospel*. Revised and enlarged. Nashville: Abingdon, 1979.

———. "Glimpses into the History of the Johannine Community." In *L'Évangile de Jean*, pp. 149-175. Edited by M. deJonge. Gembloux: Duculot, 1977.

Meeks, W. *The Prophet-King: Moses Traditions and the Johannine Christology*. Leiden: Brill, 1967.

———. "The Man from Heaven in Johannine Sectarianism," *Journal of Biblical Literature* 91 (1972), pp. 44-72.

Minear, P. *John: The Martyr's Gospel*. New York: Pilgrim Press, 1984.

———. "The Audience of the Fourth Evangelist," *Interpretation* 31 (1977), pp. 339-354.

———. "The Original Functions of John 21," *Journal of Biblical Literature* 102 (1983), pp. 85-98.

Neyrey, J. *An Ideology of Revolt: John's Christology in Social-Science Perspective*. Minneapolis: Fortress, 1988.

O'Day, G. *Revelation in the Fourth Gospel: Narrative Mode and Theological Claim*. Minneapolis: Fortress, 1986.

Okure, T. *The Johannine Approach to Mission*. Tubingen: Mohr, 1988.

Perkins, P. *The Gospel According to John*. In *The New Jerome Biblical Commentary*. Edited by R. Brown, J. Fitzmyer, and R. Murphy. Englewood Cliffs: Prentice-Hall, 1990.

Pesch, R. *Der reiche Fishfang (Lk 5:1-11/Jo 21:1-14)*. Dusseldorf: Patmos, 1969.

Rensberger, D. *Johannine Faith and Liberating Community.* Philadelphia: Westminster, 1988.

Robinson, J. *The Priority of John.* London: SCM, 1985.

————. "The Destination and Purpose of St. John's Gospel." In *New Testament Studies*, pp. 107-125. London: SCM: 1984.

————. " 'His Witness is True': A Test of the Johannine Claim." In *Twelve More New Testament Studies*, pp. 112-137 London: SCM, 1984.

Rosenblatt, M-E. "The Voice of the One Who Prays in John 17." In *Scripture and Prayer,* pp. 131-144. Edited by C. Osiek and D. Senior. Collegeville: Liturgical Press, 1988.

Sanders, J. *A Commentary on the Gospel According to St. John.* Edited and completed by B. Mastin. London: Black, 1968.

Schlatter, A. *Der Evangelist Johannes.* 3d. ed. Stuttgart: Calwer, 1960.

Schnackenburg, R. *The Gospel According to St. John.* 3 vols. Translated by K. Smyth and others. New York: Crossroad, 1990.

————. *Das Johannesevangelium: Erganzende Auglegungen und Exkurse.* Freiburg: Herder, 1984.

————. "Das Johannesevangelium als hermeneutische Frage," *New Testament Studies* 13 (1966-67), pp. 197-210.

Senior, D. *The Passion of Jesus in the Gospel of John.* Collegeville: Liturgical Press, 1991.

Segovia, F. *Love Relationships in the Johannine Tradition.* Atlanta: Knox, 1982.

————. " 'Peace I Leave with You; My Peace I Give to You': Discipleship in the Fourth Gospel." In *Discipleship in the New Testament*, pp. 76-102. Edited by F. Segovia. Minneapolis: Fortress, 1985.

Shepherd, M. "The Jews in the Gospel of John: Another Level of Meaning," *Anglican Theological Review*, Supplementary Series 3 (1974), pp. 95-112.

Sherwin-White, A. N. "The Trial of Christ." In *Historicity and Chronology in the New Testament*, pp. 97-116. Edited by D. Nineham et al. London: SPCK, 1965.

Sloyan, G. *John.* Atlanta: Knox, 1988.

Smalley, S. *John: Evangelist and Interpreter.* Exeter: Pater Noster, 1978.

————. "The Sign in John XXI," *New Testament Studies* 20 (1974), pp. 275-288.

Smith, D. M. *Johannine Christianity: Essays on its Setting, Sources, and Theology.* Columbia: University of South Carolina, 1984.

————. *John.* Minneapolis: Fortress, 1976.

————. "The Presentation of Jesus in the Fourth Gospel," *Interpretation* 31 (1977), pp. 367-378.

Thompson, M. *The Humanity of Jesus in the Fourth Gospel.* Minneapolis: Fortress, 1988.

Thyen, H. "Entwicklungen innerhalb der johanneischen Theologie und Kirche im Spiegel von Joh 21 und der Lieblingsjüngertexte des Evangeliums." In *L'Évangile de Jean*, pp. 259-299. Edited by M. deJonge. Gembloux: Duculot, 1977.

von Wahlde, U. *The Earliest Version of John's Gospel.* Collegeville: Liturgical Press, 1989.

————. "The Johannine 'Jews': A Critical Survey," *New Testament Studies* 28 (1981-82), pp. 33-60.

Vouga, F. *Le cadre historique et l'intention théologique de Jean.* Paris: Beauchesne, 1977.

————. "The Johannine School: A Gnostic Tradition in Primitive Christianity," *Biblica* 69 (1988).

Wengst, K. *Bedrangte Gemeinde und verherrlichter Christus.* Neukirchen-Vluyn: Neukirchener Verlag, 1983.

Westcott, B. F. *The Gospel According to St. John.* 2 vols. London: Murray, 1881.

Yee, G. *Jewish Feasts and the Gospel of John.* Collegeville: Liturgical Press, 1989.

Zahn, T. *Das Evangelium des Johannes.* Wuppertal: Brockhaus, 1983 reprint.

Index of Names and Subjects

Index of Modern Authors

Index of Scriptural References

I John